Highlights &
Sidelights
of the
CIVIL WAR

Highlights & Sidelights of the
CIVIL WAR

Philip Dorf

Southfarm Press

Middletown, Connecticut

This Trade Paperback Edition
is published by
SOUTHFARM PRESS
A Division of Haan Graphic Publishing Services, Ltd.
P.O. Box 1296, 8 Yellow Orange Circle
Middletown, CT 06457

By arrangement with
William H. Sadlier, Inc.

Copyright ©1989 by Oxford Book Company, Inc.
A Division of William H. Sadlier, Inc.
Home Office: 11 Park Place, New York, NY 10007

Cover design copyright ©1989 by
Haan Graphic Publishing Services, Ltd.

All rights reserved, which includes the right to reproduce
this book or portions thereof in any form whatsoever.
For information address Southfarm Press,
P.O. Box 1296, Middletown, CT 06457

ISBN: 0-913337-16-1
Library of Congress Catalog Card Number: 89-60308

First Printing: April, 1989
Printed in the United States of America

This work was previously published as part of
So Rich A Story by Philip Dorf; copyright ©1969 by
Oxford Book Company, Inc.

Contents

	Foreword	7
Chapter 1:	Slavery Splits the Nation	9
Chapter 2:	The Road to War	18
Chapter 3:	The House Divided	37
Chapter 4:	Downfall of the Confederacy	52
Chapter 5:	Assassination and Attempted Assassination	79
	Index	87

Illustrations in this edition are courtesy of: Dover Publications, Inc., pages 23 *left* (engraving by John C. Buttre), 25 (engraving on left by George E. Perine), 29 *right*, 40 *upper left*, 40 *middle left* (after ambrotype by Matthew Brady), 40 *middle right* (engraving by John C. Buttre), 40 *bottom left* (engraving by H. W. Smith), 40 *bottom right* (engraving by John C. Buttre from a photograph by Matthew Brady), 44 *upper right*, 44 *middle left*, 44 *middle right* (engraving by Alexander H. Ritchie), 63 *right*; Illinois State Historical Library, page 81; Library of Congress, pages 10 (Daguerreotype by Matthew Brady), 29 *left* (Brady-Handy Collection), 44 *bottom left* (Brady Collection), 44 *bottom right* (Brady-Handy Collection), 56, 57, 63 *left* (Brady-Handy Collection); Mercaldo Archives, page 23 *right*; National Archives, Brady Collection, page 13; New York Historical Society, page 40 *upper right*, 44 *upper left*, 78; United States Navy, page 59; Wanda P. Haan, Page 85.

Cover illustrations courtesy of — Library of Congress, Brady-Handy Collection: Robert E. Lee *(left)*; Dover Publications, Inc.: U. S. Grant *(left center)*; National Archives, Brady Collection: Jefferson Davis *(right center)*; Dover Publications, Inc., Engraving by H. B. Hall's Sons: Abraham Lincoln *(right)*.

Foreword

Highlights & Sidelights of The Civil War is designed primarily to accent the drama, faith, sacrifice, humor, and heartbreak of The Civil War Period.

Without facts history may become an old wife's tale; yet facts alone are not enough. The story of America's Civil War should stir interest, not smother it and should pulsate with spirit, not statistics.

Facts need not, however, rule out the emotions. There is a proper place in The Civil War Story for the incidents, anecdotes, and digressions which add color and flavor to the record.

The appropriate human-interest story will throw light on a person and The Civil War Era.

An anecdote, a couplet from a 19th century poem or song, a slogan, catchword, or epigram, a memorable phrase from a speech or an editorial — all these are vital threads in the intricate tapestry of Civil War history.

They reveal the manners and morals of the age; they reconstruct its tempo and mood. They mirror the ambitions, follies, and hopes of Abraham Lincoln's and Jefferson Davis's generation. They provide the accompaniment to the chronicle of its failures and, more important, its achievements.

A people's traditions constitute the bedrock of national existence. And upon this foundation may depend not only its prospect of greatness, but even its hope of survival. More than a century ago, Edward Everett (1794 – 1865), U.S. Senator and Millard Fillmore's Secretary of State, said: "And how is the spirit of a free people to be formed and animated and cheered, but out of the storehouse of its historic recollections?"

Highlights & Sidelights of The Civil War aims to provide one key to this storehouse about a critical period in our history.

1

SLAVERY SPLITS THE NATION

For in a warm climate no man will labor for himself who can make another labor for him.

— *Thomas Jefferson (1787)*

The "peculiar institution" becomes a Southern institution: Originally Thomas Jefferson's Ordinance of 1784 for the Southwest – trans-Allegheny territories ceded to the Federal government – contained a clause prohibiting slavery after 1800. Had this clause remained, slavery would have been confined to the South Atlantic states; but the Congress of the Confederation struck it out. In the Northwest Territory, slavery was barred by the Ordinance of 1787. In the meantime, it was being eliminated from the Northeast, where it had never taken firm hold. The backwoodsmen of Vermont (in the 1777 Constitution for the Republic of Vermont) were the first to ban slavery; and when a would-be slave-owner applied for a writ to protect his "property" the judge asked, "Do you have a bill of sale from God Almighty?"

Enlightened Southerners took the lead in suppressing the overseas slave trade. To Edward Rutledge of South Carolina, Jefferson wrote on July 14, 1787, "This abomination must have an end. And there is a superior bench reserved in heaven for those who hasten it." At Philadelphia, James Madison urged that the new Congress be free to prohibit further importation at once, but he had to accept a 20-year delay. Washington hoped we would soon become a "confederacy of free states," and Jefferson supported the program of settling liberated slaves in West Africa which led to the founding of Liberia. "It is still in our power," he wrote, "to direct the process of emancipation and deportation peaceably." He was mistaken. Mounting demand for fiber made cotton-growing the South's most important enterprise. To grow cotton profitably Southerners believed they had to have slave labor.

John C. Calhoun's political career included being a U.S. Senator, Secretary of War, Secretary of State, and Vice-President of the U.S. Though he was a spokesman of the planter aristocracy in the south, he came originally from the back-country small-farmer class. As a boy, he worked the fields alongside slaves.

The plantation system: Conditions on southern plantations varied from state to state, and from lowlands to upland areas. Senator Macon of North Carolina was an upland tobacco-grower who, at times, labored in the fields at the head of his slaves. John C. Calhoun, spokesman of the planter aristocracy, came originally from the back-country small-farmer class. A slave boyhood companion later recalled, "Many's the time me and Marse John has plowed together."

The cotton-growing districts required new hands, and without any deliberate planning Virginia, Kentucky, and other tobacco-growing states became a "slave-breeding" section for the deep South. On Virginia and Maryland plantations it was not unusual for slave women to bear a dozen or more children. The life of the slave in the cotton and rice districts was less tolerable than in the border states; he worked harder, received poorer food and clothing, and was ruled by an overseer rather than by a patriarchal master. This implanted in slaves in the border states a horror of being "sold down the river."

The most deplorable feature of the slave auction (or private sale) was not so much the break-up of families as the sale of humans as if they were cattle. It was an age in which dispersal of people was a common occurrence; European immigrants left their families, as did

West-bound settlers and gold-seekers. But in nearly every instance the individual retained freedom of decision. The misery of the slave stemmed from his helplessness, as John Greenleaf Whittier made clear in the "Lament of the Virginia Slave Mother."

> Gone, gone – sold and gone
> To the rice-swamps dark and lone
> From Virginia's hills and waters.
> Woe is me, my stolen daughters!

Household slaves held a preferred position. While traveling in Georgia the British geologist Charles Lyell once asked a black woman whether she belonged to a certain family. "Yes, I belong to them," she replied, "and they belong to me."

Household slaves generally were sticklers for etiquette. One day Lyell was touring the countryside with his planter host when their carriage stopped. The black coachman had discovered he had dropped one of his white gloves. They drove back slowly for about a mile – still no glove – then the master with a gesture of resignation drew off his own gloves and handed them to his slave. "When our charioteer had deliberately put them on," Lyell wrote, "we started again."

The emancipation problem: A prime field hand in 1850 cost about $1,000. His owner ran many risks of losing this capital for the slave might run away, die, or become incapacitated. Southern slave-owners often hired white laborers for such hazardous jobs as repairing a roof or steeple. Public opinion required the planter to look after sick, injured, and aged slaves, while self-interest dictated care of field hands even when work was slack. In a sense, he provided social security for his slaves at a time when the Northern mill-owner had no responsibility for his hands.

Henry Clay, a border-state planter and slave-owner, in time arrived at a practical solution to the slavery problem: purchase and emancipation of slave children at birth. Ralph Waldo Emerson went one step further – emancipation of all slaves by purchase. Fanatics on both sides prevented so sane a solution. Aside from the sacrifice of life, had the South set free all slaves without compensation the cost would have been a fraction of the property damage of the Civil War; and had the Federal government bought (and freed) every slave the cost would have been only a fraction of the money spent in crushing the Confederacy.

Reminiscences of a former slave-owner: After the Civil War, Henry Ravenal of South Carolina set down some recollections of slavery:

On marriage – If they married at home there was no impediment to their union for life. If they married the slave of another, there was the liability to separation from various causes over which there might be no control.

Among some, the marriage was duly solemnized by the Christian ministers of the churches around; and in such cases, separation was forbidden. Among others, this ceremony was left with the black preachers who used their own forms, and separation was permitted.

On family discipline – Their family discipline was very loose, often going from extremes of laxity to unnecessary severity. Old Maum Market had a large family. (The old slave nurse was known as "Mauma" or "Maum", not "Mammy" as Tin Pan Alley has it.)

One day when I saw her administering a flagellation on one of the boys, the other ran off to hide. I inquired what he was afraid of, if he had done nothing wrong. He replied, "You don't know ma. When he lik one, he lik all. He say if we dont want um now, we want um tomorrow – so he lik now for save time."

On respect for property – Sometimes the barn would be robbed or the sweet potato cellar would be opened and a few bushels taken out. Heavy robberies and burglaries were all but unknown.

No man can degrade another without . . . : Slavery meant despotism on one side and submission on the other; the growing number of mulatto slaves in the South testified to the corroding influence of the "peculiar institution."

Historian Rhodes has some frank pages on relations between masters and attractive female slaves. At auctions a handsome mulatto or quadroon girl – "suitable for house servant" – often brought double the price of a field hand. Attorney Salmon P. Chase (later Secretary of the Treasury) once received a letter from a Georgia planter begging him to arrange for the emancipation and the placing in foster homes of three mulatto children he had sent to Ohio. "The too familiar case," commented biographer A. B. Hart, "of a father seeking to get his own flesh and blood out of bondage."

Harriet Martineau talked with an Alabama slave who had repeatedly run away from the kindest of masters, and concluded that what he wanted was to be free of any master. To the Southern argu-

As a congressman, Representative Howell Cobb of Georgia had stated, "A fire had been kindled which ... only seas of blood can extinguish." Cobb went on to be Governor of Georgia, Secretary of the Treasury under President Buchanan, and an organizer of the Confederacy.

ment that slavery had lifted the slave out of African slavery, and that he was lucky to have someone to look after him, Northerners sometimes cited this anecdote: A fugitive slave was being questioned by an Ohio judge. Was his master harsh? Did he overwork him? Give him little to eat? The prisoner shook his head in the negative. "You had a good kind master," the judge said. "I don't see why the devil you wished to run away." "Well, Judge," the fugitive replied, "I left the situation down dar open. You kin go right down and git it."

A fire has been kindled . . .: The first sectional clash over slavery in the territories came in 1818 when Missouri applied for admission as a slave state. After two years of wrangling, a compromise was reached, but no one believed it was a permanent solution. In April, 1820 – forty-one years before Fort Sumter – Jefferson wrote, "But this momentous question, like a firebell in the night, awakened and filled me with terror. I considered it at once as the knell of the Union. It is hushed, indeed, for the moment. But this is a reprieve only, not a final sentence." And Representative Howell Cobb of Georgia prophesied, "A fire had been kindled which . . . only seas of blood can extinguish."

Speak as the trumpet does – sterner and stronger: Whittier denounced all compromise on slavery and demanded its complete eradication. But abolitionism was not limited to Northerners. James Birney, a Kentuckian by birth and a one-time Alabama planter, settled in Cincinnati where he printed an abolitionist newspaper, the *Philanthropist*. Two sisters, Sarah and Angelina Grimke of Charleston, South Carolina, moved to Philadelphia where Angelina published an "Appeal to the Christian Women of the South."

Besides Whittier, well-known Northerners who were drawn to abolitionism included the feminist leader Lucretia Mott, Horace Greeley of the *New York Tribune,* Gerrit Smith of New York, David Wilmot of Pennsylvania, and Chase of Ohio. Most abolitionists were earnest, benevolent, peaceable men and women. But, as is true of most crusades, the movement also attracted fanatics like William Lloyd Garrison, Elijah P. Lovejoy, and John Brown.

With the first issue of the *Liberator* (January 1, 1831) Garrison, a printer by trade, took command of radical abolitionism. His challenge was to anti-slavery moderates as well as pro-slavery extremists. "Tell the mother to gradually extricate her babe from the fire into which it has fallen," he wrote, "but urge me not to use moderation in a cause like the present."

Emerson, who condemned the Garrisonians as "wrong-headed," conceded they were "wrong-headed in the right direction." But historian C. W. Thompson says flatly that "Garrison and his little band were a drag on the wheel; and that but for them slavery might have been abolished sooner and more easily."

At first there was almost as great an outcry against Garrison in the North as in the South. On October 21, 1838, he was attacked by a Boston mob – later called the Broadcloth Mob because it included so many reputable well-dressed citizens – and dragged through the streets. He was saved from serious injury or death by being lodged temporarily in jail where he was safe from the fury of the mob.

Other riots occurred in the North. Some were touched off by a hot-headed visiting English abolitionist, George Thompson, who urged the slaves (who possessed neither leaders nor arms) to rise against their masters. At Alton, Illinois, the intemperate abolitionist editorials of Elijah P. Lovejoy provoked a clash in which the editor and one of the attackers were killed. At Cincinnati, Birney's printing shop was sacked.

Because the Constitution sanctioned slavery, Garrison denounced it – later publicly burning a copy – and advocated dissolution of the Union. More moderate antislavery elements organized the Liberty Party and named Birney for President in 1840; they were, however, no more popular that the radicals. The doorway of many a Liberty Party member was bespattered with tar or black paint.

The sword suspended over the South: The threat of a slave insurrection haunted Southerners. Even during colonial days, when the number of slaves was small, there had been uprisings (for example, the Cato revolt in South Carolina in 1739).

In 1831 in Southampton County, Virginia, Nat Turner's insurrection took the lives of more than 60 whites, chiefly women and children, before it was crushed. As in earlier uprisings every slave directly involved was executed. Shocked by the revolt, the South adopted sterner measures. Slaves were forbidden to possess firearms, to beat drums or blow horns lest these be employed as signals, to be out of quarters after dark, to assemble at night unless a white person was present, or to leave the plantation without a pass.

Since some copies of the *Liberator* penetrated the Mason and Dixon line, most Southern states now forbade teaching any slave to read and write. Where instruction could still be given by the owner, as in Virginia, public opinion discouraged it. Resourceful slaves, however, managed to pick up their letters.

The well-known orator and journalist Frederick Douglass, a slave in Maryland until 1838 when he escaped to the North, disclosed, "When I met with any [white] boy I knew could write, I would . . . make the letters which I had been so fortunate as to learn and ask him to beat that. In this way I got a good many lessons in writing."

Not all Northern communities favored educating the slave. In Canterbury, Connecticut, Prudence Crandall was jailed for opening her school to black children. And there were other forms of discrimination. . . . Southern Congressmen, in 1836, secured passage of a House resolution tabling all petitions relating to slavery without debate. Though not an abolitionist, Congressman John Quincy Adams fought the action as a violation of the First Amendment. The "gag resolution" boomeranged, for it coupled slavery with limitation on freedom of speech and the right of petition. When after years of protest the "Old Man Eloquent" in December, 1844, secured its repeal, he entered in his diary, "Blessed, forever blessed be the name of God!"

A lone Southern voice is heard and spurned: Angered and alarmed by abolitionism, the South became more militant. Abolitionists who crossed the Mason and Dixon line were jailed or driven back. Southern postmasters refused to deliver abolitionist literature; Southern legislatures prohibited the printing of anti-slavery material; Southern public opinion frowned on criticism of slavery. It was conform – or get out!

In 1857, Hinton R. Helper of North Carolina published *The Impending Crisis*, an indictment of slavery from an economic standpoint. No friend of the blacks – he wanted them shipped off to Africa – Helper argued that slavery kept the non-slave-holding white majority subservient to the planter minority and was responsible for the relatively low level of Southern agriculture, industry, and even culture. But the time for a reasonable approach had passed. Southern legislatures banned Helper's book, and more than one Southerner swore to shoot the author on sight.

Another reprieve – the Compromise of 1850: Though politicians tried to ignore the problem of slavery in the territories acquired from Mexico, this issue – along with the South's demand for a more effective fugitive slave law and the North's insistence upon abolition of slavery in the nation's capital – could no longer be evaded. In December, 1849, the break-up of the Union appeared imminent. "We have in the legislative bodies of this Capitol and in the States," Clay said, "twenty-odd furnaces in full blast, emitting heat and passion and intemperance." Though he represented Missouri, a border slave state, doughty old Senator Benton was a nationalist – reason enough for Southern extremists to denounce him. During one debate Senator Foote of Mississippi made an insulting remark, and when the aroused Missourian advanced threateningly Foote drew a loaded revolver. As other Senators stepped between them, Benton cried out, "I am not armed . . . Stand aside and let the assassin fire." A committee of investigation reported sadly, "No similar scene has ever been witnessed in the Senate of the United States." Far worse lay ahead.

Anti-slavery leaders at first spurned Clay's compromise as "sentiment for the North and substance for the South"; yet in the South the compromise was denounced as "cowardly." Benton assembled some Fourth-of-July toasts indicative of secession sentiment in 1850: "The Union: Once a holy alliance, now an accursed bond.". . ."Disunion rather than degradation.". . ."The American Eagle: In the event of a dissolution of the Union, the South claims as her portion the heart of the noble bird; to the Yankees we leave the feathers and carcass."

California – distant, lusty, and growing – boldly drew up a state constitution barring slavery and by her move speeded acceptance of the Compromise. California's stand seemed puzzling, for labor was scarce and many of the gold-seekers came from the South. An old mountaineer gave this explanation: "In a country where every white man makes a slave of himself there's no sense in keeping Negroes."

The passing of the Big Three: The debates on the Compromise of 1850 marked the last appearance in the Senate of Calhoun, Clay, and Daniel Webster. The Senate's roster for this session also included Benton of Missouri, Houston of Texas, Jefferson Davis of Mississippi, Stephen Douglas of Illinois, Chase of Ohio, Seward of New York, and others – a galaxy of stars.

Calhoun, who demanded the opening of all U.S. territories to slave-owners, was so ill that his last speech to the Senate (March 4, 1850) had to be read for him by a colleague. Four weeks later he lay dead. Frail and feeble-voiced, Clay told the Senate, "I am here, expecting soon to go hence, and owning no responsibility but to my own conscience and to God." (The Kentuckian died in Washington on June 29, 1852.) Though Webster had long opposed extension of slavery, he supported the Compromise in his famous Seventh-of-March Address as preferable to disunion and war. Anti-slavery leaders now accused him of sacrificing principle to win Southern support for his Presidential ambitions, and termed him a "Benedict Arnold" and a "Judas." In "Ichabod" Whittier mourned:

> So fallen! so lost! the light withdrawn
>   Which once he wore!
> The glory from his gray hairs gone
>   For evermore.

Whittier was mistaken. Posterity has attributed Webster's Seventh-of-March speech to patriotism; at any rate, he did not live to see the outcome of the next Presidential election. Webster was at Marshfield, on the Massachusetts coast, when he realized the end was near. One of his last requests was that his sailboat be moored so that the Stars and Stripes at the masthead would be visible from his sickbed. He died on October 24, 1852. "A great man with a small ambition," was Emerson's judgment – yet our democracy requires that great men aspire to the Presidency.

In 1957, a committee of the U.S. Senate, charged with selecting five outstanding Senators to be honored by portraits in the Senate Reception Room, presented this list: Robert A. Taft of Ohio, Robert M. LaFollette of Wisconsin, and Clay, Calhoun, and Webster – the "Big Three" of the 1820-1850 era.

2

THE ROAD TO WAR

A house divided against itself cannot stand. I believe this government cannot endure permanently half slave and half free.

— *Abraham Lincoln (1858)*

The Fugitive Slave Act a festering sore: With enactment of the Compromise of 1850 Southern planters and Northern mill-owners breathed a sigh of relief, for dissolution of the Union would have been costly for both. "Cotton thread holds the nation together," Emerson observed: but this "thread" at once was subjected to enormous strain by the Fugitive Slave Act of 1850, the one part of the Compromise the North could not swallow. Presently the Concord philosopher was writing defiantly, "I will not obey it, by God!"

A fugitive slave law was no innovation. The Constitution provided that persons held to service or labor in one state escaping into another "shall be delivered up on claim of the party to whom such service or labor may be due," and Congress, in 1793, had passed a Fugitive Slave Act. The South's insistence on a more stringent measure was a blunder, for in one year the new act made more converts to the anti-slavery cause than abolitionists had made in 25 years.

The law denied persons accused of being fugitive slaves the right of trial by jury. Vermont, Massachusetts, and Michigan promptly enacted "personal liberty" laws which in effect nullified the Federal act. Another form of nullification was direct action by Northerners. At Syracuse (New York) a black mechanic, Jerry, who had been lodged in jail pending trial as a fugitive slave, was forcibly released (and sent to Canada) by a mob led by Congressman Gerrit Smith and the Rev. Samuel J. May. Near Oberlin (Ohio) an apprehended Negro was rescued by an armed crowd which included a Sunday school superintendent and a college professor.

In May, 1854, a fugitive slave, Anthony Burns, was arrested in Boston. At the moment New England was seething because of the Nebraska Bill and a visiting Southerner observed, "If the bill should be passed, the Fugitive slave law is a dead letter throughout New England. As easily could a law prohibiting the eating of codfish and pumpkin pies be enforced as that law be executed." He had gauged the situation correctly; it required a battalion of artillery, 4 platoons of marines, 22 companies of Massachusetts militia, the police, and a marshall's *civil posse* to escort Burns to the wharf where a U.S. revenue cutter was waiting to take him to Virginia. The *Richmond Enquirer* commented, "A few more such victories and the South is undone."

Free blacks in the North united to keep fellow-blacks from being returned to bondage. Near Christiana (Pennsylvania) two fugitives took refuge in the house of a black. When a party led by their former master, Dr. Gorsuch of Baltimore, surrounded the house, a horn summoned other blacks to the scene and in the ensuing fight Dr. Gorsuch was killed. Though 35 persons were arrested, all were released for no jury would indict them.

Tales of the "Underground": The Act of 1850 resulted in an expansion of the "Underground Railroad," a movement to help runaway slaves reach free Canada; the "conductors" on the "road," otherwise law-abiding citizens, were banded together to circumvent the Federal law and outwit the slave-catchers. In the mid-West network Oberlin, Ohio, became an important station. Sneering at Oberlin's zeal, a neighboring town indicated its direction not by the customary index finger, but by the figure of a hard-running fugitive. Escaping slaves took heart when they saw that guide board.

Accounts of narrow escapes and clever ruses circulated from one "depot" to another. One slave couple traveled openly by train from the deep South until they reached the free states. The woman, a light-colored mulatto who had disguised herself as a young man, passed for white and her husband acted as her servant. At inns, travelers had to sign registers and she couldn't write, but she got around this by carrying her arm in a sling, explaining that she had injured it in an accident.

The book of the century: It was frankly a moral tract, in the form of a novel, inspired by indignation over the Fugitive Slave Act. Its structure had flaws; its literary style was commonplace, its language sometimes trite, its humor forced, its situations occasionally tinged with sentimentalism. Yet, it was written with such sincerity and was so successful in baring the injustice of slavery, that the work – *Uncle Tom's Cabin* – became the most influential book ever written in America.

Facts and figures: *Full Title:* Uncle Tom's Cabin: A Tale of Life Among the Lowly. *Author:* Mrs. Harriet Beecher Stowe, a daughter of Puritan New England; her father was a minister, as was her husband and later her sons. *Publication:* After serialization in the antislavery *Washington National Era,* it was issued in book form on March 20, 1852, by J.P. Jewett of Boston. *Sales:* First year – 300,000 copies; ultimately, at least 6,000,000 in regular editions. *Longevity:* In 1889 it still led the fiction list at the New York circulating library. *The Play:* More people saw the dramatization than ever read the book; as late as 1890 scores of traveling troupes were still giving performances throughout the nation. *Recognition abroad:* In England the novel was reviewed by Macaulay; in France, by George Sand; in Germany, by Heine. In time the book was translated into every important foreign language.

Mrs. Stowe had never lived in the South, but had visited Kentucky and for 18 years resided in Cincinnati where she came in contact with the "Underground." Except for Simon Legree, the slaveholders she portrayed were just, generous, and amiable – she was indicting a system rather than individuals. Recognizing the part New England traders had played in transporting slaves to America she cast Simon Legree – now a synonym for brutal bullying – as a son of New England. The opening scene of *Uncle Tom's Cabin* was criticized, for it showed a Kentucky gentleman (Mr. Shelby) entertaining at table a slave trader (Haley). This was a slip on Mrs. Stowe's part. Lincoln was better informed: he knew that the slave dealer was despised by the planters. In his 1854 speech at Peoria, Illinois, he said, addressing himself to Southerners: "It is common with you to join hands with the men you meet; but with the slave dealer you avoid the ceremony – instinctively shrinking from the snaky contact."

A memorable slave "auction" in Brooklyn: One of Mrs. Stowe's brothers, the Rev. Henry Ward Beecher, pastor of Plymouth Church in Brooklyn, gave his congregation a dramatic lesson in the practices of slavery. On Sunday, June 1, 1856, he held a mock auction: the "parcel," a mulatto slave girl, Sarah. "She was bought by a slave-trader for twelve hundred dollars," Beecher explained, "and he has offered to give you the opportunity of purchasing her freedom. She has given her word of honor to return to Richmond if the money is not raised." Then imitating an auctioneer's patter the minister cried: "Stand up Sarah!. . .Now look at her trim figure!. . .How much do you bid?" At the question assistants began circulating baskets for contributions. Given this emotional setting – with half the fashionable congregation in tears – it is no wonder that not only was the $1,200 raised but enough over to buy a home for Sarah. Other slave-redeeming sales were held in the North.

Another dark horse wins the Presidency: Millard Fillmore, who had become President on Taylor's death, was intelligent and able, but anti-slavery Whigs, who never forgave him for signing the Fugitive Slave Act, belittled him and blocked his nomination in 1852. A story of the day concerned a carriage which, it was asserted, Fillmore wanted to buy from a resident of Washington. Accompanied by Edward, the White House doorkeeper, the President went to look at it. The rig seemed to be in fine shape, but at the last moment Fillmore said to Edward, "Will it do for the President of the United States to ride in a second-hand carriage?" "Sure, your Excellency," Edward replied, "You're only a siccond-hand Prisident, you know."

Cass of Michigan again was the leading Democratic candidate but his squatter-sovereignty doctrine had made enemies on both sides of the slavery issue, and on the 49th ballot the Democratic Convention finally chose a compromise candidate, Franklin Pierce of New Hampshire. The Whigs topped this, needing 53 ballots to nominate General Winfield Scott. Pierce once had been a hard drinker, and though he had long since mastered the habit the Whig press ignored this and referred to him as "the hero of many a well-fought bottle."

Pierce's margin over Scott – 254 electoral votes to 42 – foreshadowed the end of the Whig party. The youngest man (48) who up to that time had assumed the Presidency, Pierce began his Inaugural Address with a moving reference to the recent death in a railroad accident of his last surviving child, a boy of 13.

Kansas – prelude to civil war: Pierce hoped that the slavery controversy was "forever at rest," but it soon blazed forth anew over the Kansas-Nebraska Act. Sponsored by Senator Stephen A. Douglas of Illinois, it repealed the Missouri Compromise insofar as it applied to that part of the Louisiana Territory not yet admitted to statehood. And it organized this area into two territories (Kansas and Nebraska) on the principle of squatter sovereignty – the people of the territories to decide whether to bar slavery. The Civil War might have occurred even had the Nebraska Bill been defeated, but it is certain that its enactment hastened its onset. Short and thickset in appearance, able and dynamic in debate, Douglas was called the

"Little Giant" by his followers. His opponents were less complimentary: some Ohio ladies sent the Senator 30 pieces of silver; since his middle name was Arnold comparisons with that other Arnold were inevitable.

In theory a democratic solution of the problem of slavery in the territories, squatter sovereignty in practice was a tragic failure. Kansas became a battleground with bullets far more persuasive than ballots. Strangers approached one another warily, rifle or pistol in hand. When Governor Reeder received the returns of the 1855 election of a Kansas territorial legislature, he was flanked by an armed bodyguard, and his own loaded pistols lay before him. New Englanders formed the vanguard of the Northern emigrants to Kansas. For them Whittier wrote:

> We cross the prairie, as of old
> The Pilgrims crossed the sea,
> To make the West as they the East
> The homestead of the free.

When at a public meeting in a New Haven (Connecticut) church the leader of a group of Kansas-bound emigrants said they needed, not Bibles, but Sharp's rifles, the Rev. Beecher assured those present that if they would subscribe to 25 rifles his church would provide the rest. Thereafter, the rifles of Northern emigrants were termed "Beecher's Bibles."

A new party is born: The disintegration of the Whig party was completed by the Nebraska Act; and at first it seemed that its place would be taken by a secret society, "The Sons of '76," or the "Order of the Star-Spangled Banner." This was in effect a Protestant League opposed to rising Catholic immigration and influence; among other things it demanded that only native Americans be eligible for public office. Since members replied, "I know nothing," when asked about their secret organization it was soon dubbed the Know-Nothing-Party. (In derision opponents formed a Know-Something Society.) Entering politics, Know-Nothing leaders designated their order the "American Party," but so sophomoric and biased a dark-lantern organization could not long remain a major political force.

In 1854, Northern anti-slavery Whigs united with anti-slavery Democrats, disillusioned Know-Nothing members, and remnants of the Liberty Party and the Free Soil Party to form a new Republican Party opposed to further extension of slavery. Nominating John C.

John Fremont (left) was the first Republican Party candidate for President, running in 1856. Among the charges leveled at Fremont by the Democrats, who had nominated James Buchanan for President, was that much of his fame as an explorer of the Rocky Mountains was due to his excellent guides, such as Kit Carson (right).

Fremont for President, in 1856, the Republicans demanded admission of Kansas as a free state. "Free speech, free soil, and Fremont" made an attractive campaign slogan. The Democrats named a "safe" candidate, James Buchanan of Pennsylvania.

Born in Georgia and reared in South Carolina, the 43-year-old Fremont was a citizen of California and an opponent of slavery. Again the campaign hoop-la almost obscured the real issues. Since Fremont was a Rocky Mountain explorer, his followers erected "Rocky Mountain Huts" and staged torch-light parades led by ax-bearing "mountaineers." Democrats charged that much of Fremont's reputation as a "Pathfinder" was built on his excellent guides, notably the famed Kit Carson. Emulating the custom of early explorers, Fremont once had cut a large cross on a rock. Led by the Know-Nothing press the opposition called him a Catholic and, therefore, "the tool of the Pope and the Jesuits." (Fremont disclosed that he and his wife were Episcopalians, but that their marriage had been performed by a Catholic priest.) It is doubtful whether the religious angle had an effect on the outcome. Fremont had a good build-up and made a fine appearance, but in view of his later mediocre career Republicans were lucky that he didn't win in 1856.

Fremont's wife, Jessie – vivacious, popular, and politically minded – was the daughter of Thomas Hart Benton. Though he adored his daughter and admired her husband, Benton, an old-fashioned Jacksonian Unionist, would not support a sectional party and voted for Buchanan.

A bachelor, the new President-elect had come in for considerable ribbing during the campaign. One Republican song ran: "Old bachelors are low in rate . . .They'd never populate a state."

Violence spreads to the halls of Congress: Buchanan's election settled nothing, and "Bleeding Kansas" remained on the critical list. In 1857 a pro-slavery territorial legislature called for a constitutional convention. With free-staters boycotting the Lecompton Convention on the ground that the ballot boxes had been stuffed, the pro-slavery party put through a clause protecting *existing slave property* if further admission ever was prohibited. In the meantime, violence had spread from Kansas to the Capitol.

In May, 1856, in a lurid speech "The Crime Against Kansas," Senator Sumner of Massachusetts described the policy pursued up to that time as "the rape of a virgin territory compelling it to the hateful embrace of slavery." Continuing in this turgid vein Sumner next turned his oratory on elderly Senator Butler of South Carolina. A few days later, while at his desk in the Senate – the day's session was over – Sumner was suddenly attacked by Preston Brooks (Congressman from South Carolina and Senator Butler's kinsman) and so severely beaten with a heavy gutta-percha cane that the injuries nearly proved fatal.

Sumner's philippic had been disgraceful; Brooks's reprisal was cowardly. Yet each section saw only its own side of the controversy. When Sumner's term expired, the Massachusetts legislature re-elected him, and his empty seat in the Senate bore mute witness to the sectional passions. Rejoicing that an "abolitionist" had been chastised, the South toasted Brooks and presented him with numerous canes to replace the one he had broken on Sumner's head. A House motion to expel Brooks failed to get the necessary two-thirds majority; certain of vindication at home he resigned his seat, and was immediately re-elected.

Postscripts: Brooks died in January, 1857, and Butler in May. After undergoing treatment abroad for his injured spine, Sumner recovered and returned to the Senate. Despite an immense conceit he was an able man and later became Senate leader of the Radical-Republican majority.

A case that became a cause célèbre: In the autumn of 1846 an illiterate Missouri slave "signed" his name to a petition initiating a suit for freedom. Nearly 11 years later – after consideration by the courts

Senator Charles Sumner of Massachusetts (left) was attacked in the senate by Representative Preston Brooks of South Carolina (right). Brooks beat Sumner with a cane repeatedly, almost killing him because of his views on slavery.

of Missouri and the lower Federal courts – the U.S. Supreme Court ruled against the petitioner. Since the plaintiff was a descendant of black slaves, Chief Justice Taney declared he was not a citizen and ineligible, therefore, to sue in a Federal court. In judicial records the case is labeled *Scott vs. Sandford;* history calls it the "Dred Scott Decision" – the most momentous ruling ever handed down by the Supreme Court.

Born in Virginia, Dred Scott had been sold to Dr. John Emerson, an army surgeon, who had taken him from Missouri to Illinois, then to Minnesota Territory, and finally back to Missouri. The suit for freedom argued that residence on free soil north of 36° 30', before repeal of the Missouri Compromise, had emancipated him. A pawn in the sectional conflict, Scott was assured of freedom regardless of the outcome of the case. In 1857 he was technically the property of John Sandford of New York, a brother of Dr. Emerson's widow. The latter had remarried; and since her second husband, Dr. Chaffee of Springfield, was a member of Congress, title to Scott had been transfered to Sandford to avoid involving the name of an anti-slavery Congressman from Massachusetts in the ownership of a slave in Missouri.

Had the decision that Scott could not bring suit in a Federal court stopped there the case would have aroused little interest. But Chief Justice Taney, a Southerner, believed – as did President Buchanan, a Northerner – that a basic court ruling on the question of slavery in the territories would quiet the North-South controversy. Therefore, in an *obiter dictum* the Court held that since property rights were guaranteed by the Constitution, Congress could not prohibit a citizen from taking slave property into any U.S. territory; consequently, the Missouri Compromise of 1820 had been unconstitutional and all remaining territories of the United States were open to slave-holders. The South was jubilant; the North stunned.

At Chicago, an Illinois Republican summed up his party's position: "We mean to reverse it, and we mean to do it peaceably." (Less than three years later the speaker was sworn in as President; under his leadership the Dred Scott decision was reversed, and if it was not done peaceably surely this was not Abraham Lincoln's fault.)

Democracy at the grass-roots level: Instead of quieting the agitation over slavery, the Dred Scott Decision itself engendered bitter controversy. While campaigning for re-election in 1858, Senator Douglas of Illinois was challenged to debate the burning issue by his Republican opponent, Abraham Lincoln. Douglas did not underestimate his challenger. "I shall have my hands full," he said. "He is the strong man of his party – full of wit, facts, dates – the best stump speaker, with his droll ways, in the West." In the series of seven debates, held in various parts of the state, the contestants spoke from the same platform, and the press and the telegraph carried their words to every corner of the land.

The Court had ruled that Congress could not bar slave-holders from a U.S. territory – did not this (Lincoln asked) nullify the Kansas-Nebraska Act? With an eye on the Presidency, Douglas said it was possible to accept the Dred Scott Decision without abandoning squatter sovereignty. If it was unconstitutional for Congress to bar slavery from a territory, Lincoln replied, was it not also illegal for a territorial legislature receiving its powers from Congress? Could water rise higher than its source? It was down-to-earth probing, but Douglas was an agile debater. No matter how the courts interpreted the "abstract question" of slavery, he said at Freeport, the people of a territory could exclude it by hostile "police legislation." Did this mean, Lincoln countered, that a thing *legally* could be driven away from a place where it had a *legal* right to be? Though Douglas narrowly won re-election to the Senate, his attempt to straddle the slavery issue alienated many Northerners, while antagonizing the South, and probably cost him the Presidency in 1860.

After his defeat, Lincoln said he felt like the boy who had stumped his toe – "it hurt too bad to laugh and he was too big to cry." He was sure that he would now "sink out of view" and be forgotten. Yet, hardheaded Republican politicians were already sizing up reaction to the debates, were beginning to measure the gaunt, awkward, prairie "sucker" by the paramount yardstick of politics – votes. Lincoln himself soon modified his view of the 1858 result. Applying a wrestling term he said, "It's a slip, and not a fall."

The strength of the land was in him . . . : As the drama of slavery and sectionalism moves toward its climax, it is time to take a closer look at the man cast by destiny as its principal actor, the leader whose martyrdom capped a nation's agony. A reporter asked Lincoln about his early life. "It can all be condensed," he replied, "into a single sentence, and that sentence you will find in Gray's *Elegy* – 'the short and simple annals of the poor.'"

Born in a Kentucky log cabin, and brought up in the hard poverty of the Illinois frontier, the youth became expert at butchering hogs. He excelled at wrestling where his height, long reach, and rawboned leanness were an advantage; he knew the feel of an ax. In later life Lincoln said he obtained his scanty schooling "by littles." When he came to fill out a form for the Congressional Directory, next to the item "Education" he wrote, "Defective."

At 22 young Lincoln had taken charge of a country store at New Salem, Illinois. Once, discovering that he had overcharged a customer 6 cents, he tramped two miles to return the sum. This, and scrupulous care in weighing and measuring, earned him the handle – as the saying went on the frontier – of "Honest Abe." He opened a grocery store in partnership with a man named Berry. The business went downhill, and when Berry died Lincoln was saddled with a debt of several hundred dollars. He managed to clear it off.

Politics was as much a part of the raw, hustling, growing Midwest as the ring of the ax or the tangy aroma of burning logs. Lincoln started early: at 23 he ran for a seat in the Illinois legislature, and in his first speech is reported to have said, "I am humble Abraham Lincoln. My politics are short and sweet, like the old woman's dance . . . If elected I shall be thankful; if not it will be all the same." It proved to be "all the same," but two years later he won and served several terms.

During one campaign, Whig friends made up a purse of $200 for expenses. After his election Lincoln returned $199.25. "I did not need the money," he explained. "I made the canvass on my own horse, my entertainment, being at the houses of friends, cost me nothing; and my only outlay was 75 cents for a barrel of cider which some farmhands insisted I should treat them to."

Biographers have been fascinated by the romantic chapters of Lincoln's life: the tender, elusive love affair with Ann Rutledge, cut short by her death of malaria; the engagement with Mary Owen, broken when that robust lady returned his ring; finally the "on-again, off-again, on-again" courting of the highspirited Mary Todd. Writing in November, 1842, to a fellow-attorney about two lawsuits, Lincoln added almost as an afterthought: "Nothing new here, except my marrying, which, to me, is a matter of profound wonder."

He was by this time a rising lawyer in Springfield, raw capital of a frontier state. He had attended no law school, for in that day a man could get his license by reading law in an attorney's office or even at home. Lincoln never became "learned" in the law – still he managed to win one case after another. He had the knack of getting at the heart of a suit, of bringing the homely wisdom of a rural society to bear upon complex legal issues. He once said, "If I can strip this case of technicalities and swing it to the jury I'll win it." In court, as in the country store, he remained "Honest Abe." Half-way through one trial, on discovering that his client was deceiving him, Lincoln disappeared. When a messenger finally located him, Lincoln said, "Tell the Judge that I can't come; my hands are dirty."

In his youth, Lincoln had helped take a flatboat down the Mississippi and at New Orleans had seen a slave sold at public auction. Profoundly disturbed he had said to a companion, "If I ever get a chance to hit that thing [slavery] I'll hit it hard." But not until the Nebraska Act did he throw himself into the movement to check further expansion of slavery.

The raid of midnight terror: He was a fanatic – a throwback to some hard, unsmiling Puritan in Cromwell's army who had killed Cavaliers with a "holy" zeal, an iron-willed old man who was sure he was God's chosen instrument to free the slaves. He was John Brown, *Pottawatomie Brown*, who had killed, and risked being killed, in Kansas. For Garrison and his followers he had nothing but contempt: "These men are all talk." In secret Brown hatched his desperate plan, then struck suddenly. His plan failed – how could it have succeeded? – but the attempt brought the nation one step closer to the war out of which emancipation was to come.

Abolitionist John Brown (left) sought to enlist the support of black leader Frederick Douglass (right) for his attack on the Federal arsenal at Harpers Ferry, Virginia. Douglass was horrified and warned Brown that he would be trapped.

With funds provided by abolitionists, Brown secretly had purchased 200 rifles, 200 revolvers, and 950 pikes. ("Give a slave a pike and you make him a man," he said.) His objective was Harpers Ferry, Virginia, site of an old Federal arsenal where he believed were stored 100,000 to 200,000 guns – enough for a black army. At Chambersburg (Pennsylvania), where he received the arms shipped to him, Brown sought to enlist the support of Frederick Douglass. But the black leader was horrified. "You not only attack Virginia," he said, "but you attack the Federal government. Furthermore, you are going into a perfect steel trap." It was a waste of sound advice.

As is often true of rash enterprises, the initial moves were successful. On the night of October 16, 1859, Brown seized the B. & O. railroad bridge across the Potomac and wrested the Harpers Ferry armory and arsenal from its sleepy civilian watchmen. At 1:30 a.m. the first casualty of the raid occurred. When Brown's outposts stopped the southbound train, a railway porter went out to see what was wrong. Ignoring an order to halt he turned to run back – and was shot and mortally wounded; he was a free black man.

At dawn the startled citizens of the town assembled to do battle with the invaders; and at mid-day the arrival from Charlestown of a company of Virginia militia sealed Brown's fate. The exchange of shots killed or mortally wounded several on both sides, including two of Brown's sons and Mayor Beekham of Harpers Ferry. The following day a detachment of U.S. marines commanded by Colonel

Robert E. Lee and Lieutenant J.E.B. Stuart, battered down the door of the engine-house and beat down further resistance. Brown himself received head and body wounds.

John Brown pays the penalty: "The plan was the attempt of a fanatic or madman which could only end in failure," Lee reported to the War Department. But the whole South was in a fever: everywhere men stood guard to prevent any new outbreak. Brown was turned over to the Virginia authorities and tried for murder, for men had been killed in the raid. When counsel assigned to him began a plea of insanity, the wounded prisoner stopped him. Having failed to free the slaves by force, the militant abolitionist welcomed the chance to publicize his fight against slavery (as he put it) "by hanging for a few minutes by the neck." Found guilty of treason and murder, the prisoner was sentenced to be hanged.

"Old Brown," warned Edmund C. Stedman in the New York *World*, "may trouble you more than ever when you have nailed his coffin down." But Virginia was troubled only by a possible rescue attempt, and on the day of the execution (December 2, 1859) Charlestown swarmed with armed militia. (Serving in the Jefferson Guards was a private, John Wilkes Booth. The groundwork was being laid for another deed of mad fanaticism.) As the trap-door of the scaffold was sprung, a Colonel Preston cried out "So perish all such enemies of Virginia! All such enemies of the Union! All such foes of the human race!"

With the horrors of the 1857 Sepoy Mutiny in India fresh in people's minds, it is doubtful whether a dozen men could have been found in the South on that day who did not echo Colonel Preston's words. But in the North, Whittier wrote, "Not the raid of midnight terror, but the thought which underlies."

And in his private journal Longfellow entered, "They are leading Old John Brown to execution in Virginia for attempting to rescue slaves. This is sowing the wind to reap the whirlwind which will soon come."

The mounting fever: After Brown's raid, Northerners planning to go South for the winter were advised to go instead to the West Indies, or to southern Europe, to avoid being insulted. Congress assembled in December, 1859, but one member who did not resume his seat was Senator Broderick of California. In that distant state the Kansas issue had split the Democratic Party, with Broderick leading the free-state wing and Judge Terry of the California Supreme Court the pro-slavery faction.

A crack shot, Terry resigned his post and challenged Broderick to a duel. At the signal the inexperienced Broderick pressed too soon and his bullet hit the ground; taking aim Terry then mortally wounded his opponent. (Years later Terry threatened U.S. Supreme Court Justice Field and was shot dead by a marshall assigned to protect the Justice.)

The madness spread. In April, 1860, Representative Lovejoy, brother of the abolitionist who had been killed in 1837, made a vitriolic anti-slavery speech which set off a near riot. "So far as I know," Senator Hammond of South Carolina remarked, "every man in both houses is armed with a revolver – some with two." Soon afterward, as if in corroboration, a New York Congressman grew so vehement in debate that his pistol accidentally fell from his coat to the floor of the Chamber. Reports of such incidents, coupled with the wildest of rumors, kept the South in a fever of excitement. From the day of the raid (though Brown was not a Republican) "Republican" was a nasty epithet there. It was in this surcharged atmosphere that the nation prepared for the most critical election in its history.

A self-styled "sucker" is nominated for President: A speech at Cooper Union, New York (February 27, 1860), was the crucial moment of Lincoln's career. To the critical Easterners the first impression was not too favorable: on the platform a tall, awkward, homely man, clad in ill-fitting clothes, speaking in a high-pitched voice. But by the time Lincoln had concluded with the memorable words, "Let us have faith that right makes might; and in that faith let us to the end dare to do our duty as we understand it," the packed audience had forgotten his unprepossessing appearance. Horace Greeley said, "That's the most powerful speech I ever heard."

When the Republican Convention assembled in the huge "Wigwam" at Chicago, William H. Seward of New York seemed to have the inside track for the nomination. But the party's close-mouthed, close-calculating politicians decided that because of his obscurity before 1858 Lincoln had made fewer enemies than Seward. At Auburn, his home town, Seward was waiting for word of his selection; instead the telegraph tapped out "Lincoln." When not one of his disappointed associates seemed able to compose the conventional close-the-ranks editorial endorsing the candidate, Seward himself wrote it for Auburn's evening paper.

On May 19, a committee of the Convention arrived at Springfield to notify Lincoln formally of his selection. After a brief reply the nominee greeted the delegates individually. Pausing before Kelly of

Pennsylvania, Lincoln said, "You are a tall man, Judge. What is your height?" When Kelly gave it as, "Six-feet-three," Lincoln said, "I beat you. I am six-four without my high-heeled boots."

"Pennsylvania bows to Illinois," Kelly replied. "I am glad that we have found a candidate for the Presidency whom we can look up to."

An election which triggered a revolution: The 1860 campaign was waged on a low level. Though split on vital issues Southern Democratic journals joined Northern papers in ridiculing Lincoln's appearance – as if a beauty contest were being decided. A Charleston paper which supported Breckenridge concluded its uncomplimentary remarks about Lincoln's face and figure with "Faugh!" A Boston journal which supported Douglas fired this shaft at the Republican nominee:

> Any lie you tell, we'll swallow –
> Swallow any kind of mixture;
> But oh! don't, we beg and pray you
> Don't, for land's sake, show his picture!

Yet Lincoln's campaign picture (by Brady) has strength and dignity. Replying to the charge that Lincoln was inexperienced Lowell wrote, "He has had experience enough in public affairs to make him a statesman and not enough to make him a politician." Actually, the election had been decided before the campaign got under way. At Charleston in April, 1860, the Democratic Convention had split on the slavery question and adjourned to meet at Baltimore in June; but neither time nor a new location could heal the breach. The two rival factions adopted separate platforms and named separate candidates: Douglas by the Northern wing; Breckenridge of Kentucky by the Southern. Though Douglas dominated the campaign he could do no more than reduce the size of the popular vote cast for Republican electors.

In Washington, at midnight of November 8, 1860, the ringing of bells announced Lincoln's victory. The wife of Captain Eugene McLean (a Marylander who sympathized with the South) noted this fact in her diary, adding, "For the first time I hear disunion openly avowed and feel as much shocked as if the existence of God were denied." In the space of a semicolon, however, the lady concluded, "but reflection and history teach me there is nothing inherently divine in republics."

The South had served notice that it would never accept "a Black

Republican President." As in Jackson's day, South Carolina, a little pepperpot of a state, took the lead: On December 20, 1860, a special convention at Charleston voted to dissolve "the union now subsisting between South Carolina and other States under the name of 'The United States of America.'" Six other states of the deep South soon followed her out of the Union. While prudent Northern merchants and bankers began to suspend credit to the cotton states, secessionists in Washington, nerveless capital of a disintegrating nation, jubilantly toasted each new withdrawal.

When Mississippi went out Mrs. McLean observed, "The tall, handsome, and belligerent Mississippi woman in ecstasies." Florida was next, then Alabama . . .Georgia . . .Louisiana . . .Texas. One month before Lincoln's inauguration, delegates from the "Cotton Kingdom" drew up a constitution for the Confederate States of America and chose as President Jefferson Davis of Mississippi.

Strong sentiment against secession existed in the upland areas of Georgia and North Carolina, but Union men could not counter the argument, "We can obtain better terms out of the Union than in it." The terms of course referred to slavery, for the South feared that a Republican administration would not only bar further extension of slavery, but wipe it out entirely.

"You seek to outlaw $4,000,000,000 of property of our people." cried Senator Toombs of Georgia. "Is not that a cause of war?" Earlier, replying to Northern businessmen who urged a moratorium on further discussion of slavery, Lowell had said, "To be told that we ought not to agitate the question of slavery, when it is that which is forever agitating us, is like telling a man with the fever and ague on him to stop shaking, and he will be cured."

Let the erring sisters go their way: At the first shock of secession, some Northerners urged, "let them go that we can be a free country." Many believed that the Southern states would soon return. In "Brother Jonathan's Lament for Sister Carolina," Holmes wrote:

> Go, then, our rash sister! afar and aloof,
> Run wild in the sunshine away from our roof;
> But when your heart aches and your feet have grown sore,
> Remember the pathway that leads to our door!

Recalling Jackson's handling of the nullification crisis, others, however, condemned the "do-nothing" policy of the outgoing administration. Secretary of State Lewis Cass, old but far from feeble, had urged that the Federal forts in Charleston Harbor be re-enforced, and when President Buchanan took no action Cass resigned. "Too bad that a man has to break his sword twice in a lifetime," a Senator remarked.

Too late for peacemakers: In a last-minute compromise effort Crittenden of Kentucky proposed that the 36° 30' line of the Missouri Compromise be restored by constitutional amendment and extended to remaining territories of the United States. Southern fire-eaters ignored the white-haired Senator, while President-elect Lincoln and other Republicans refused to scrap the main plank of their party's platform. (Crittenden's family reflected the split in his state: son George fought for the Confederacy; son Thomas, for the Union. Each became a major-general.)

To assure Southerners there would be no interference with slavery where it was legal, moderates in Congress proposed a constitutional amendment – it would have been the 13th – denying to Congress the power to abolish or interfere with a state's domestic institutions, "including that of persons held to labor or service by the laws of said state." This resolution was approved by both houses of Congress and ratified by 3 states before the guns blasted it into oblivion. (When a 13th Amendment finally was added to the Constitution – in 1865 – it abolished slavery.)

There was another proposal for heading off civil war: Secretary of State Seward advised the President to pick a quarrel with Spain and France, who were threatening to intervene in Santo Domingo and Mexico respectively, in the hope that the shock of foreign war might restore internal unity. Lincoln tabled the reckless suggestion.

Mr. Lincoln comes to Washington: The President-elect and Mrs. Lincoln journeyed leisurely by rail from Springfield to Washington. At one town Lincoln kissed a little girl who by letter had urged him to grow a beard. "You see," he said, "I have let these whiskers grow for you, Grace." (The *New York Tribune* headed the story, "Old Abe Kissed by a Pretty Girl.")

But the holiday atmosphere was abruptly dissipated by rumors of an assassination plot. Secretly the President-elect's itinerary was changed. From Harrisburg, Lincoln returned to Philadelphia and proceeded directly to Washington, arriving at the capital at the hour he was scheduled to be in Baltimore. When this became known an imaginative newspaper reporter dressed up the story by inventing a disguise for Lincoln – a Scotch cap and long military cloak.

On the evening of March 2 the President-elect and Mrs. Lincoln held a brief reception in the Willard Hotel. The critical correspondent of the *London Times* noted in his diary: "There entered, with a shambly, loose, irregular, almost unsteady gait, a tall, lank, lean man, considerably over six feet in height, with stooping shoulders, long pendulous arms terminating in hands of extraordinary dimensions which, however, were far exceeded in proportion by his feet." On entering the Parlor, his wife on his arm, Lincoln said, "Ladies and gentlemen, permit me to present to you the long and the short of the Presidency." As he said "the long," he bowed, and as he said "short" he looked down at Mrs. Lincoln and smiled. Then and there one Republican editor decided that Lincoln was a "simple Susan."

Installing the sixteenth President of the United States: To forestall any secessionist interference with Lincoln's inauguration, troops patrolled Washington on March 4, 1861, but everything proceeded quietly. Buchanan accompanied the President-elect to the Capitol, and as the two stepped into the carriage a military band struck up "Dixie." It emphasized Lincoln's determination to consider himself President of the entire nation.

For the solemn occasion Lincoln wore brand-new clothes. In one hand he carried an ebony cane, the gift of an admirer; in the other, a tall glossy hat. On the platform Lincoln found a corner into which to push his cane, but could not find a place for his stovepipe hat. Thereupon, Senator Douglas, who was seated on the aisle nearby, came to the rescue and held the topper until his old rival had taken the oath and completed his address. (On May 1, 1861, at Chicago, Douglas delivered a speech urging every American "to rally 'round the flag." Then sick and worn-out, though only 48, he took to his bed and died on June 3.)

Many who had wondered whether Lincoln was "equal to the occasion" felt more reassured after his address. For its clarity and sincerity, its blend of conciliation and firmness, and its nobility of thought and phrasing the *First Inaugural* ranks as one of history's great orations.

"I shall take care, as the Constitution itself expressly enjoins upon me, that the laws of the Union be faithfully executed in all the States . . . One section of our country believes slavery is right and ought to be extended, while the other believes it is wrong and ought not to be extended. This is the only substantial dispute. . . . In your hands, my dissatisfied fellow-country-men, and not in mine, is the momentous issue of civil war. The government will not assail you. You can have no conflict without being yourselves the aggressors. . . . We are not enemies, but friends. We must not be enemies. Though passion may have strained, it must not break our bonds of affection. The mystic chords of memory, stretching from every battlefield and patriot grave to every living heart and hearthstone all over this broad land, will yet swell the chorus of the Union, when again touched, as surely they will be, by the better angels of our nature."

The Inauguration Ball was a dull affair. Mrs. McLean observed that "the *haut ton* did not come out because the Lincolns are not yet the fashion." Since the President did not dance he had ample opportunity to shake hands with well-wishers. To a reporter he said, "This is harder work than rail-splitting."

3

THE HOUSE DIVIDED

Secession! Peaceable secession! Sir, your eyes and mine are never destined to see that miracle.

— *Daniel Webster (1831)*

At Charleston where the revolution had commenced: Lincoln's policy at first seemed to differ little from Buchanan's. The new President, who was busy with details and beset by job-seekers, was getting the feel of office; besides, it seemed wise to avoid action which might drive Virginia and other border slave states into the Confederacy. Had he not said there would be no conflict unless the secessionists were the aggressors?

April 12, 1861, brought the first act of aggression – before dawn Confederate forces under General Beauregard opened fire on Fort Sumter, a Federal fortress in Charleston Harbor. Now Lincoln could appeal for volunteers to suppress the rebellion confident that the North would answer his call. Though the cannonnading lasted 34 hours, not a man on either side was lost; and despite heavy damage to the fort, it was lack of ammunition which finally compelled Major Anderson to haul down his flag.

Edmund Ruffin and Abner Doubleday fired the first shots in the Civil War. Ruffin, a Virginia planter who had pioneered in the use of marl to restore worn-out soils, was so rabidly secessionist that even Virginia could not stand him, so he went to South Carolina. There the frail old man, wearing a black hat with a secession cockade, was given the honor of firing the first cannon at Fort Sumter. At Bull Run he again fired the first gun. As the Confederacy's needs grew, Ruffin mortgaged his estates to support the cause. In June, 1865, when it had become a lost cause, the old warrior of 71 shot himself.

Doubleday's history was a happier one. He served throughout the war, surviving both Antietam and Gettysburg and attaining the rank of brigadier-general, and later gained fame as the "inventor" of modern baseball.

To Arms! To Arms!: The conflict which began at Fort Sumter has been called most generally, the *Civil War;* officially, the *War of the Rebellion;* in the South, the *War Between the States;* by one noted historian, the *War for Southern Independence,* and by another, the *Second American Revolution.* It was all these – it was also the *Needless American Tragedy.* The United States was the only great nation which broke in two and fought a civil war over the problem of slavery.

The day after Sumter's fall Lincoln called for 75,000 volunteers to serve for three months in suppressing the rebellion; on May 3, he appealed for 42,000 more, this time three-year men. The firing on Fort Sumter galvanized the North into action: broadsides, newspaper notices, and handbills shouted the dread word WAR! – gave the command TO ARMS! – announced the time and place for organizing companies of MILITIA! In the Confederacy the same call was being sounded, and merchants and plantation owners, mechanics and hill-country farmers, were falling in under a new banner.

Throughout the war Washington was in peril of seizure by the Confederates. On the south lay Virginia which seceded after Lincoln's call for troops; with a telescope, Lincoln's young secretary, John Hay, could see the Confederate flag on a rooftop in Alexandria. On the north was Maryland, a slave state, which though it did not secede contained thousands of sympathizers with the South.

A Philadelphia company of militia hastened to the defense of the capital, but it was almost entirely without arms. Better prepared was the Massachusetts Sixth Volunteers which reached Baltimore on April 19. While transferring from one railroad station to another the troops were mobbed: four soldiers were killed and 36 wounded; 12 of the rioters were killed and an indeterminate number wounded.

The first bloodshed of the war was shed, to America's sorrow, on the anniversary of the battle of Lexington. Not until other regiments from New York and New England had broken Baltimore's blockade was Washington safe.

Amateurs at war: America long had boasted that its citizens were prepared for peace not war. Both sides hastily improvised uniforms and equipment, dug up old military manuals, and sent abroad for weapons to supplement their stock of arms.

At Washington, barracks were lacking. Finding the Willard jammed, Kansas volunteers made "camp" in the East Room of the White House. Massachusetts troops were quartered in the Capitol and young Hay, on looking into the Senate Chamber, found a "throng of bright-looking Yankee boys . . . scattered over the desks, chairs, and galleries, some loafing, many writing letters." Civilians as well as soldiers went about armed.

In Richmond the scene was much the same. "The street immediately in front of this hotel," Mrs. McLean wrote, "is the drill-ground for a South Carolina company, and it is one of my occupations to see how naturally these polka-dancing young men take to the 'double-quick.'" (For lack of space we say goodbye at this point to the gallant and perceptive Mrs. McLean and her diary.)

Yes, they were amateurs and no doubt their early maneuvers amused Europe's professional militarists. Since they did not long remain amateurs it will do no harm to note one or two episodes. Near Fortress Monroe two Federal regiments inadvertently opened fire on one another – fortunately their marksmanship was poor – and then retreated; not knowing what was going on, the Confederates also prudently withdrew. This was the "battle" of Big Bethel. At Vienna (Virginia) some green Union troops boarded a train for a reconnaissance. When the cars were fired upon, the soldiers took to the woods and on reaching camp reported they had been turned back by enemy "masked batteries."

Score one for the Confederacy: By July, 1861, Washington could no longer ignore the North's war-cry: Forward to Richmond! Besides, the term of many of the three-month volunteers was about to expire. On Sunday, July 21, McDowell's Union army attacked Beauregard's forces at Bull Run (or Manassas). So certain were Washington residents of victory that many drove out in carriages and buggies to see "the show." Monday morning Northern journals were reporting, "The Rebels Crushed." This was like taking the first-half score of a football game for the final result, for in mid-afternoon the arrival of reinforcements under Joseph E. Johnston had enabled the Confederates to turn the tables. When some units fell back, McDowell's army took panic and fled pell-mell until it reached the fortifications south of the Potomac.

In an effort to cover up defeat some Northern papers hinted that General McDowell was drunk. The truth is the general took nothing but water. (In youth McDowell had attended a French military school where he had been given so much sour wine that he developed an aversion to alcohol in any form.) Others in the North suggested that the Union defeat was a well-merited punishment from the Almighty for having attacked on the Sabbath.

A President in search of a general: As Commander-in-Chief it

General Irvin McDowell

General George B. McClellan

General John Pope

General Ambrose E. Burnside

General Joseph Hooker

General George G. Meade

UNION GENERALS

was Lincoln's responsibility to approve basic war strategy, provide men and materials, and select the generals.

Exit McDowell – enter McClellan: Only 34, "Little Mac" was an able drillmaster – the Army of the Potomac was never stampeded again – but he was also vain, ambitious, and over-cautious. On October 10 the General said to Lincoln, "Don't let them hurry me is all I ask." Months passed and McClellan still was not ready. Daily the press reported, "All quiet on the Potomac," until the phrase became a byword. Even Lincoln's patience began to wear thin. Conceding that the general was an excellent military engineer, he thought it unfortunate that he had "a special talent for a stationary machine."

Exasperated because the President and Secretary of War Stanton wanted frequent detailed reports, McClellan once sent Lincoln a dispatch, "Have just captured six cows. What shall we do with them?" Back came the reply, "Milk them." Refusing to take offense the President said, "I will hold McClellan's stirrup for him if he will only win us victories."

Spring came, but McClellan still delayed – the roads were bad. (Later, in his *Memoirs*, the General related an anecdote without really getting its point. He once asked a Cossack officer who had fought against Napoleon how the roads were in those days. "My son," the aged veteran said, "in war the roads are always bad.") Finally the Union commander began to move his army of 100,000 men against Richmond – but so slowly that the Confederates gradually were able to build up their forces. After its victory at Fair Oaks (May 31-June 1) the Army of the Potomac could see the spires of Richmond, 6 miles away, and hear St. John's church bells. But the swampy terrain of the Chickahominy valley prevented a direct advance with heavy artillery.

Exit McClellan – enter Pope: After Fair Oaks, the Union general faced two master strategists, Lee and his lieutenant "Stonewall" Jackson. Since he had been in his class at West Point, Jackson knew McClellan's abilities and shortcomings, and Lee was able to plan accordingly. Out-maneuvered in the hard-fought Seven Days' Battles of the Peninsular Campaign, McClellan retreated. Pope now took command. In a return engagement at Bull Run the Union army suffered another defeat.

Exit Pope – re-enter McClellan: When Lee invaded Maryland, Lincoln recalled "Little Mac." At Antietam (September 17, 1862), the bloodiest one-day battle of the war, the Union army stopped the invaders. But McClellan spent 19 days making up his mind to cross the Potomac, then 9 days in crossing – and Lee got away.

Exit McClellan – enter Burnside: This time "Little Mac's" removal was final. Where his predecessor had been cautious to a degree of timidity, Burnside was impetuous to the point of recklessness.

Fredericksburg (December 13, 1862) was a slaughter of Union troops against impregnable Confederate positions. (In a later campaign Burnside was holding Knoxville, Tennessee. An aide told the President firing was reported from that vicinity. Replying that he felt much relieved, Lincoln added that anything indicating Burnside had not been overwhelmed was cheering. "Like Sally Carter, when she heard one of her children squall, would say: 'There goes one of my young ones – not dead yet, bless the lord.'")

Exit Burnside – enter Hooker: If Lincoln joked, it was to cover up his heartache. After Fredericksburg the North was in despair: enlistments fell off while desertions snow-balled; some families sent their men at the front parcels containing civilian clothing. "End this murderous holocaust," Stedman of the *New York World* pleaded, "Shall all our offering be in vain? Abraham Lincoln, give us a MAN!"

At last they thought they had their MAN in Hooker. "Fighting Joe" was the very picture of a general: "A tall and statuesque form – grand fighting head and grizzled russet hair – red, florid cheeks and bright-blue eyes," is the way John Hay described him. Though Hooker drank little, what he did take flushed his cheeks and was responsible for reports of his "drunkenness."

The President and "Fighting Joe": On appointing Hooker (January 26, 1863) Lincoln had written, "I have heard, in such a way as to believe it, of your recently saying that both the army and government needed a dictator . . .Only those generals who gain successes can set up dictatorship. Now what I ask of you is military success and I will risk the dictatorship."

As the months passed the risk diminished. Hooker who dashed about on horseback sometimes sent the President dispatches datelined, "Headquarters in the saddle." Said Lincoln sadly, "The trouble with Hooker is that he's got his headquarters where his hind-quarters ought to be."

Inspecting the Army of the Potomac in April, Lincoln's final words to Hooker were, "In the next battle *put in all your men.*" But at Chancellorsville (May 2-3) the Union commander kept 30,000 troops in reserve until the battle was lost. "My God," Lincoln cried, "What will the country say! What will the country say!"

Worried lest "Fighting Joe" try to redeem Chancellorsville by some rash stroke, the President wrote to him, "I would not take any risk of being entangled upon the river, like an ox jumped half over a fence and liable to be torn by dogs front and rear, without a fair chance to gore one way or kick the other." Suspecting that Lee was planning a second invasion of the North – as he was – Hooker proposed to march on Richmond. With sounder military judgment the President advised, "I think Lee's army and not Richmond is your sure objective point." Four days before Gettysburg Lincoln replaced Hooker with Meade – a last-minute gamble, but it paid off.

The Virginians: Some special quality of soil and air, along with a tradition of public service, may have accounted for Virginia's output of statesmen and soldiers. The "Old Dominion" gave the Confederacy its three top commanders: Lee, Joseph E. Johnston, and "Stonewall" Jackson. (A fourth Virginian, the methodical Thomas, never defeated in battle, remained loyal to the Union.) Paradoxically, though the state became the war's principal battleground it had only 2,184 slave owners out of a population of more than one million.

Robert E. Lee, son of a Revolutionary War cavalry general, was an honor graduate of West Point – No. 1 in his class – who had served in the U.S. Army for a quarter of a century. He considered slavery an evil, and secession a calamity, and said so even after South Carolina seceded, but when Virginia left the Union he felt he had to go along with his state. That in Lee the Confederacy had acquired its most valuable asset was not immediately recognized. Not until June 1, 1862, after Joseph E. Johnston was wounded at Fair Oaks, did Lee take command of the Army of Northern Virginia. Basically he was a defensive tactician; but necessity twice forced him to assume the offensive, since the North's superior resources would have nullified a permanent Fabian policy. Lee's two drives were staged partly to draw Union armies away from Richmond and partly in the hope that victory on Northern soil might bring foreign intervention or a negotiated peace.

Lee was more than the Confederacy's ablest general; his name became a rallying cry. Stories about Lee the man as well as the soldier – his kindness as well as firmness, his concern for the welfare of his men, his eagerness to get into the thick of the fighting ("Go back, General Lee! Go back!" his vanguard shouted at one point in the Wilderness battles) – made their way from camp and battlefield and helped shore up the South's morale in the face of growing shortages and sacrifices.

General Pierre G.T. de Beauregard

General Thomas J. "Stonewall" Jackson

General Albert S. Johnston

General Joseph E. Johnston

General George E. Pickett

General Robert E. Lee

CONFEDERATE GENERALS

In battle Lee's most effective striking arm was Thomas J. (Stonewall) Jackson. The sobriquet was earned at Bull Run when Confederate General Bell, rallying his men, cried out: "Look at Jackson! There he stands like a stone wall." In youth Jackson had led a wild life, but he changed his ways and became a puritan. Refusing to touch liquor again he said, "I am more afraid of it than of Federal bullets." His men said they could judge the size of the fight ahead by the length of time their general remained on his knees in prayer.

In battle Jackson depended upon speed and deception, employing his troops as a "foot-cavalry" in daring flanking maneuvers. On the march, Jackson did not spare himself. Biographer Freeman notes that during the Peninsular Campaign the general fell asleep one night at mess, "with his supper between his teeth."

Confronted by Hooker's larger army at Chancellorsville (May 2, 1863), Lee sent Jackson at the head of 30,000 men on a wide "end run" around the Union forces. After pushing 15 miles through tangled woods, Jackson's infantry fell upon the unsuspecting Union right and routed it. To reform his troops the general accompanied by his staff, spurred forward, but, encountering the Federal rear guard, they wheeled about; in the darkness they were taken for Federal cavalry and fired upon by their own men. Jackson fell gravely wounded; pneumonia set in and on May 10 he died.

Gettysburg – the high tide of the Confederacy: Later Lee said, "Had I Stonewall Jackson at Gettysburg I would have won a great victory." Had this occurred, in the heart of a populous Northern state, and placing both Washington and Philadelphia in peril, Lincoln would have been under great pressure to negotiate peace. For two days the great battle see-sawed. On the third day (July 3, 1863) Lee gambled, throwing Pickett's fresh division against the Union center strongly posted on Cemetery Ridge. In the face of a withering fire 15,000 Confederate veterans swept across the valley and pressed up the slope. A handful reached the crest, planted their flag among some abandoned Union cannon, and then fell back. Shouldering full responsibility for the Confederate defeat Lee said to the gallant Pickett, "Your men have done all that men could do; the fault is entirely my own."

Despite the threat of a Union counter-attack, Lee remained cool and collected. To an officer who was striking his horse for shying at the bursting of a shell he called out, "Don't whip him, Captain; don't whip him. I've got just another foolish horse myself, and whipping does no good."

General Hancock who had directed the Union defense which

shattered Pickett's charge was hit and knocked from his horse. While a surgeon was treating his wound he dictated a dispatch to General Meade urging him to press forward. "The enemy must be short of ammunition, " he pointed out, "as I was shot with a tenpenny nail." But the grizzled Union commander hesitated.

General Meade, victor in the fearful three-day battle (Union casualties, 23,003; Confederate 20,451), was a capable officer. Elevated at short notice to the command of the Army of the Potomac he did his best – and it was good enough to stop Lee. But he lacked confidence in his ability to destroy the Confederate Army ("I'm not Napoleon," he once told his staff) and failed to follow up his advantage. Lee slipped back to Virginia. "Our army held the war in the hollow of their hand," Lincoln said sadly, "and they would not close it."

A few appropriate remarks: For the dedication on November 19, 1863, of a soldiers' cemetery at Gettysburg, the Committee in charge engaged Edward Everett as orator of the day; then, almost as an afterthought, it also invited the President "to set apart formally these grounds to their sacred use by a few appropriate remarks."

The story that Lincoln jotted down his address on the back of an old envelop while on the train to Gettysburg is a myth, for the President had prepared a first draft at Washington. Everett spoke for nearly two hours, a sound scholarly address, then the President delivered the official consecration – 272 words taking about two minutes. A photographer was setting up his equipment for a picture, but before he could put his head under the hood for an exposure Lincoln was finished.

Since the press had advance copies of Everett's speech but not of Lincoln's, most papers merely reported, "The President also delivered a few appropriate remarks." In an age which expected a formal address to be garnished with allusions and quotations, Lincoln's brief speech was generally considered "flat, dull and commonplace." But there were some who dissented, and among them was Edward Everett. "I should be glad," he wrote to Lincoln, "if I could flatter myself that I came as near to the central idea of the occasion in two hours as you did in two minutes." With the graciousness that marked his personal exchanges the President replied, "In our respective parts yesterday, you could not have been excused to make a short address, nor I a long one."

"The world will little note nor long remember what we say here" is the only part of Lincoln's "remarks" which posterity has rejected.

Professor Gilbert Highet has called the *Gettysburg Address* "the best known moment of American prose."

The Mississippi, not Richmond, the key to victory: By coincidence, the day after Gettysburg the Confederate garrison of Vicksburg, 30,000 strong, surrendered to Grant, and it began to dawn on the North that the West was the decisive theater of the war. Grant and Sherman, who won their first laurels in the West, early recognized this; on the Confederate side it was grasped only by a brilliant cavalry leader, Forrest.

It is necessary to backtrack a bit. A West Pointer, Grant served in the Mexican War, but resigned from the army in 1854 to try farming and storekeeping. (More about this later.) After Sumter, he volunteered and became a colonel of an Illinois regiment. In August,1861, Lincoln who was about to appoint 36 new brigadiers asked various Northern Congressmen for suggestions. Representative Washburne of Illinois, who had seen Grant train raw volunteers, sent in his name.

After some minor successes Grant attracted national attention in February, 1862, by capturing Fort Henry on the Tennessee River. (Serving under him in this campaign was General Charles F. Smith, a veteran with dash and fire, who had been Commandant at West Point when Grant was a cadet.) From Fort Henry, he moved against Fort Donelson on the Cumberland River. When after some hard fighting Confederate General Buckner proposed a parley on terms of surrender, Grant promptly replied, "No terms except unconditional and immediate surrender can be accepted. I propose to move immediately upon your works." To the North which had long fed on promises and delays, on assurances and disappointments, "unconditional surrender" was a tonic. (Historian Bruce Catton observes that Grant's note to Buckner had an "exuberant Star-Spangled, Yankee-Doodle ring to it – put up or shut up – fight or quit.")

Hero or villain?: At Donelson the Confederacy lost nearly 15,000 men – and U.S. Grant gained a new nickname. In Grant's case this business of names may be confusing. He was christened Hiram Ulysses. As a boy he was called Ulysses ("Useless", by some neighbors who considered him a trifle backward.) The Congressman who named him to West Point, who had heard the youth referred to as Ulysses and knew his mother was a Simpson, made out the papers for "Ulysses Simpson Grant." After this it would have taken an act of Congress to set matters straight. When fellow cadets spotted Grant's initials he became "Uncle Sam" or plain "Sam." But after Donelson, it was "Unconditional Surrender" Grant.

Hoping to retrieve the ground lost at Donelson, Confederate General Albert Sidney Johnston attacked Grant at Shiloh. The fierce two-day battle (April 6-7, 1862) ended in a narrow but costly Union victory, and the Northern press charged Grant with neglecting to fortify his position. Although subjected to heavy pressure to remove him, the President stood firm. To A. K. McClure of *Century Magazine* Lincoln said, "I can't spare this man; he fights." (The able Johnston, who had felt keenly the loss of Donelson, was determined to beat Grant at Shiloh or die in the attempt. Leaving his field headquarters, the Confederate commander led the advance of a Tennessee regiment and was hit in the leg by a ball which severed an artery. It proved a mortal wound.)

And it was Vicksburg which held the key to the Mississippi: While a Union squadron "corked" the mouth of the great waterway, 2,500 troops under General Butler occupied New Orleans. Annoyed by recurring insults – one woman spat upon an officer; another from a balcony emptied a jar of slops on two officers in the street below – Butler directed that any woman who insulted a Union officer or sol-

Union gunboats, which were really converted riverboats, attacked Fort Donelson on the Cumberland River in 1862.

dier should be treated as a woman of the streets "plying her avocation." The incidents ceased, but Ben Butler – a bizarre personality, vain, tactless, and quarrelsome – was cursed from one end of the South to the other. And the South never forgot, never forgave. When Butler died in 1893 – 28 years after Appomattox – a Southern journal printed an across-the-page headline: PRAISE GOD FROM WHOM ALL BLESSINGS FLOW: THE BEAST IS DEAD.

Though the loss of New Orleans was a blow, the Confederacy still held a 200-mile stretch between Fort Hudson and Vicksburg; over this "bridge" moved Louisiana sugar, Texas grain and beef, and European munitions shipped to the Mexican port of Matamoras and then overland by way of Texas. Grant had opened the campaign against Vicksburg in January, 1863, but initial setbacks led to renewed demands that he be replaced. Specifically, his detractors charged that he drank too much. (Most historians hold that at this time Grant was not touching liquor.) When the charge was laid before Lincoln he wanted to know what brand Grant drank, explaining he wished to send a few barrels of it to other Union commanders. One gathers that Lincoln already sensed that he had found his general.

When direct assaults on Vicksburg failed, Grant turned to orthodox siege tactics. On July 3, with soldiers as well as civilians on

Union gunboats attacked Vicksburg, Mississippi on April 16, 1863. The Confederates set fire to houses and barrels of tar on both sides of the river, making the Union gunboats excellent targets.

starvation rations, General Pemberton surrendered. Hopefully Lincoln declared, "The signs look better. The Father of Waters again goes unvexed to the sea . . .Peace does not appear as distant as it did . . .It will then have been proved that among freemen there can be no successful appeal from the ballot to the bullet." But the agonizing conflict still had nearly two years to run.

Grant's star on the rise: As a reward for Vicksburg, Grant was commissioned a major-general in the regular army. Soon afterward he visited New Orleans to confer with General Banks. Knowing Grant's reputation for horsemanship (as a cadet he had been the Academy's best rider), Banks presented him with a spirited horse not yet properly broken. The courtesy nearly cost the Union the life of its ablest soldier, for as Grant mounted, the animal became frightened by a passing locomotive and bolted. The General was thrown and knocked unconscious; for weeks he had to use crutches.

In East Tennessee the fortunes of war shifted with bewildering rapidity. Rosecrans's veteran Army of the Cumberland had occupied Chattanooga and seemed to have Bragg's Confederate forces on the run. Suddenly Bragg turned, routed part of the Union army at Chickamauga and forced Rosecrans to fall back to Chattanooga. (The steadiness of the Union left wing, 25,000 troops under Thomas, gained for the general the title "Rock of Chickamauga.") Taking command in person Grant reorganized his forces, then in a desparate three-day battle (November 23-25, 1863) defeated Bragg and sent him into headlong retreat. One can sympathize with Bragg who at Chattanooga faced the Union's four top generals: Grant, Sherman, Sheridan, and Thomas – the only time these four served on one field.

In March, 1864, Grant was appointed lieutenant-general in command of all Union armies. Leaving Sherman and Thomas in the West he himself took on Lee in the death-grapple in Virginia.

The personal side of U.S. Grant: Vicksburg and Chattanooga made Grant a popular hero – Northern journals now could not give their readers enough about him. Born in Ohio, April 27, 1822, the son of a farmer who also operated a tannery and later a livery stable, young Grant became expert at breaking colts. At West Point he was an indifferent student, except in mathematics. He had no particular love for military life, having accepted appointment as a cadet because he loathed working in his father's tannery. Drill he hated – possibly because he was so tone-deaf that he had trouble keeping in step with the music. (He once said he could recognize only two tunes: "One is Yankee Doodle and the other isn't.")

In the Mexican War Grant served first under Taylor, then under Scott, and was breveted captain for gallantry at Chapultepec. After the war Grant married Julia Dent, daughter of a Missouri planter and slave-owner.

In 1854 he resigned his commission and tried farming on a backwoods tract near St. Louis. There he also dabbled in real estate, but with such meager returns that acquaintances would cross the street to avoid a request for a small loan. In 1860 he moved to Galena, Illinois, and became a clerk in his father's leather store. When war broke out the 39-year-old Grant was earning about $800 a year. No wonder friends considered him a failure.

In battle Grant's moves were based on experience and instinct rather than on a study of military science. He had a simple formula: "Find out where your enemy is; get at him as soon as you can; strike him as hard as you can, and keep moving on." What Lincoln admired most about Grant was his cool persistency. "He is not easily excited," the President said, "and he has the grip of a bulldog. Once he gets his teeth in, nothing can shake him off." In a war in which commanders on both sides deliberately exposed themselves to enemy fire, Grant became noted for his calmness in battle. In the Wilderness inferno he dismounted and sat on a stump whittling while he digested battle reports and pondered his next moves.

In appearance Grant was unprepossessing. Generally he wore a faded uniform, the stars on the shoulder of his blouse alone denoting his rank. In April, 1864, Correspondent R.H. Dana wrote that on entering Willard's Hotel in Washington he noticed a short round-shouldered man – "an ordinary, scrubby-looking man, with a slightly seedy look, as if he was out of office and on half pay, and nothing to do but hang round the entry of Willard's, cigar in mouth." Dana noted the officer's queer gait: he did not march, nor quite walk, but pitched along "as if the next step would bring him on his nose." But when Dana drew closer he saw the man had "a clear blue eye, and look of resolution as if he could not be trifled with." This was the victor of Donelson, Vicksburg, Chattanooga, and other hard-fought campaigns in the West, the new generalissimo of the armies of the Republic, the commander of nearly a million soldiers – this was U.S. Grant.

4

DOWNFALL OF THE CONFEDERACY

He is trampling out the vintage where the grapes of wrath are stored.

— Julia Ward Howe, in the "Battle Hymn of the Republic"

One war at a time: The Union blockade soon dammed up the South's exports and cut off all but a trickle of imports. At first Southerners expected Great Britain to recognize the Confederacy and force the North to lift the blockade. Pointing to cotton bales piled on the wharf at Charleston an exporter said, "There's the key that will open our ports and put us into John Bull's strong box as well."

Wheat, however, proved more vital than cotton; because of poor harvests in England and on the continent three times as much Northern grain was shipped to Britain in 1861 as in 1859, and five times as much in 1862.

"This is our affair," Lincoln said, "a family quarrel with which foreign nations must have nothing to do." Yet an over-zealous Union naval officer nearly brought about the intervention the North dreaded and the South prayed for. In the autumn of 1861 two Confederate agents, James M. Mason bound for England and John Slidell bound for France, evaded the blockade and reached Cuba. The two men sailed from Havana, November 7, on the British steamer *Trent*.

The next day the *Trent* was halted by the U.S.S. *Jacinto*, commanded by Captain Charles Wilkes; ignoring British protests Wilkes seized Mason and Slidell. While the North was jubilantly toasting Wilkes, news came from overseas: Britannia was in an uproar. The deck of a British ship on the high seas was British soil; Captain Wilkes's action, therefore, was not only a violation of international law but an affront to the Union Jack. Demanding the liberation of Mason and Slidell and "a suitable apology for the aggression,"

Queen Victoria's ministers alerted the Royal Navy, banned the export of arms and ammunition, and dispatched troops to Canada.

To a friend Lincoln earlier had said, "We fought Great Britain [in 1812] for doing just what Captain Wilkes has done. . . .We must give up these prisoners. One war at a time." Now he directed Secretary of State Seward to disavow Wilkes's act and to see that Mason and Slidell were placed aboard an east-bound British steamer. Although the North knew that the President had done the sensible thing, it resented London's tough talk and warlike preparations; and it relished Lowell's salty comment in "Jonathan and John":

> We gave the critters back, John,
>   Cos Abram thought 't was right;
> It warn't your bullying clack, John
>   Provokin' us to fight.

Washington had a grievance of its own, but was in no position to do much about it. British-made arms reached the Confederacy by way of Mexico, or by running the blockade. Again Lowell voiced the North's indignation:

> You wonder why we're hot, John?
>   Your mark wuz on the guns,
> The neutral guns, that shot, John,
>   Our brothers an' our sons.

The blighting effects of the blockade: Observing the parade of Union commanders against Lee, an American in London said, "The only real general on *our* side is General Want in the South." Before 1861 the South had produced cotton and tobacco, and had imported manufactured goods and other products. Suddenly everything was in short supply. At one time a ton of salt worth $8 at Nassau, in the nearby Bahamas, was bringing $1700 in gold (85¢ a pound) in Richmond. Substitutes for coffee included parched rye, wheat, corn, chestnuts, chickory, and cottonseed – but Southerners admitted "there was nothing like coffee but coffee." In place of tea Southerners used dried currants, blackberry and sage leaves, or the sassafras root or blossom. Opposing pickets in quiet sectors sometimes would arrange a brief "gentlemen's" truce for a brisk front-line exchange of Northern coffee and sugar for Southern tobacco.

As an ersatz quinine, Southern doctors recommended a tincture compounded of dried dogwood, poplar and willow bark, and whiskey. The Confederacy's desperate need for medicine led to smuggling from Northern cities. At Memphis, Union pickets once allowed a funeral procession to pass through the lines, quite unaware that the coffin was packed with medicines for the Confederate army. At a time when cotton piled high on Southern wharves found few buyers at 4 cents a pound it brought $2.50 a pound at Liverpool. So fantastic a spread brought into being a swarm of blockade runners. Many were intercepted by Northern warships, but those which got through earned fabulous profits. The most famous of the blockade runners, the *Robert E. Lee*, cost £32,000 in England; it ran the blockade 21 times carrying out cotton worth more than £2,000,000.

A battle which made naval history: Only once was the Northern blockade threatened. Before abandoning the Federal navy yard near Norfolk (Virginia), Union troops had set fire to the U.S.S. *Merrimac* which sank when partially consumed. The Confederates raised her, rechristened her the *Virginia,* and converted her into an ironclad armed with heavy cannon.

On March 8, 1862, this armor-plated "monster" steamed into Hampton Roads to take on the squadron of Union warships blockading the port of Norfolk. While the balls from Union ships rebounded harmlessly from her sloping iron sides, the *Merrimac* poured broadside after broadside into her wooden adversaries; she set the *Congress* on fire and then rammed the *Cumberland,* which went down with colors flying. The *Minnesota* which had run aground was helpless, but since the tide was ebbing the Confederate ironclad returned to her base, expecting to complete the work of destruction the following day. That night the Northern blockade seemed broken, for what the armored ship had done at Norfolk she presumably could do at other Southern ports.

Having earlier been apprised of the conversion of the *Merrimac,* Washington had authorized counter-measures. The following day, when the *Merrimac* steamed out to finish off the *Minnesota,* a queer affair looking like a "cheesebox on a raft" interposed itself. It was John Ericsson's *Monitor,* built at Greenpoint in Brooklyn, and it had arrived in the nick of time.

A model of simplicity, the Union ship had a revolving 11-inch-thick turret made of wrought-iron plates, mounted on an ironclad hulk whose deck was only 3 feet above water. At first glance it seemed an unequal match – the *Monitor,* 900 tons; the *Merrimac,* 3,500. But the *Monitor's* turret housed two powerful 11-inch Dahlgren guns firing an elongated 175-pound shot. For hours the ironclads pounded away at one another – at times only *10 yards apart*

– but since the armor of each was superior to the opponent's projectile neither suffered serious damage.

The British and the French, who had also been experimenting with ironclads, at once grasped the significance of the events of March 8-9. "Before the battle," the *London Times* said, "we had 149 first-class warships; we now have two."

Neither of the pioneer American ironclads ever fought again. The Confederates destroyed the *Merrimac* when they evacuated Norfolk; a gale off Cape Hatteras sank the *Monitor*. The North, however, already was building a whole fleet of ocean-going monitors. Lacking adequate ship-building and iron-making facilities the Confederacy could not match this program.

Further naval pioneering: Had the Confederacy possessed the material resources to match its naval brains the contest on the sea would not have been so one-sided. Early in the war Richmond created a Naval Torpedo Service headed by marine scientist Matthew F. Maury. In the battle of Mobile Bay (August 5, 1864) the U.S.S. *Tecumseh,* which was in the lead, hit an underwater torpedo and blew up. When the *Brookyn,* next in line, stopped and began backing up Admiral Farragut, who was lashed to a mast in the top rigging of his flagship, the *Hartford,* saw his battle array thrown into confusion.

"What's the trouble?" the *Hartford* signaled the *Brooklyn.* "Torpedoes," was the reply. "Damn the torpedoes," Farragut shouted. "Jouett, full speed!" Taking over the lead, the *Hartford* led the fleet to victory.

The Confederates also experimented with submarines. H. L. Hunley built a cigar-shaped boat driven by a propeller shaft operated manually. Four successive crews, and finally the designer himself, were lost on trial runs of the *Hunley.* But the Confederates persevered. Off Charleston, a new complement managed to sink the U.S.S. *Housatonic,* but the force of the explosion sent the metal-plated *Hunley* to the bottom along with her victim.

Confederate sea-raiders: To offset the blockade, the South unloosed swift light cruisers against Northern shipping. Some of the raiders were built in British yards in violation of international law. In the spring of 1862, the *Oreto,* out of Liverpool, emerged as the Confederate cruiser *Florida.* On learning that an even more formidable warship was nearing completion in the shipyards of Laird and Sons, U.S. Minister Charles Francis Adams placed before Foreign Secretary Russell evidence that the "290" was designed for the Confeder-

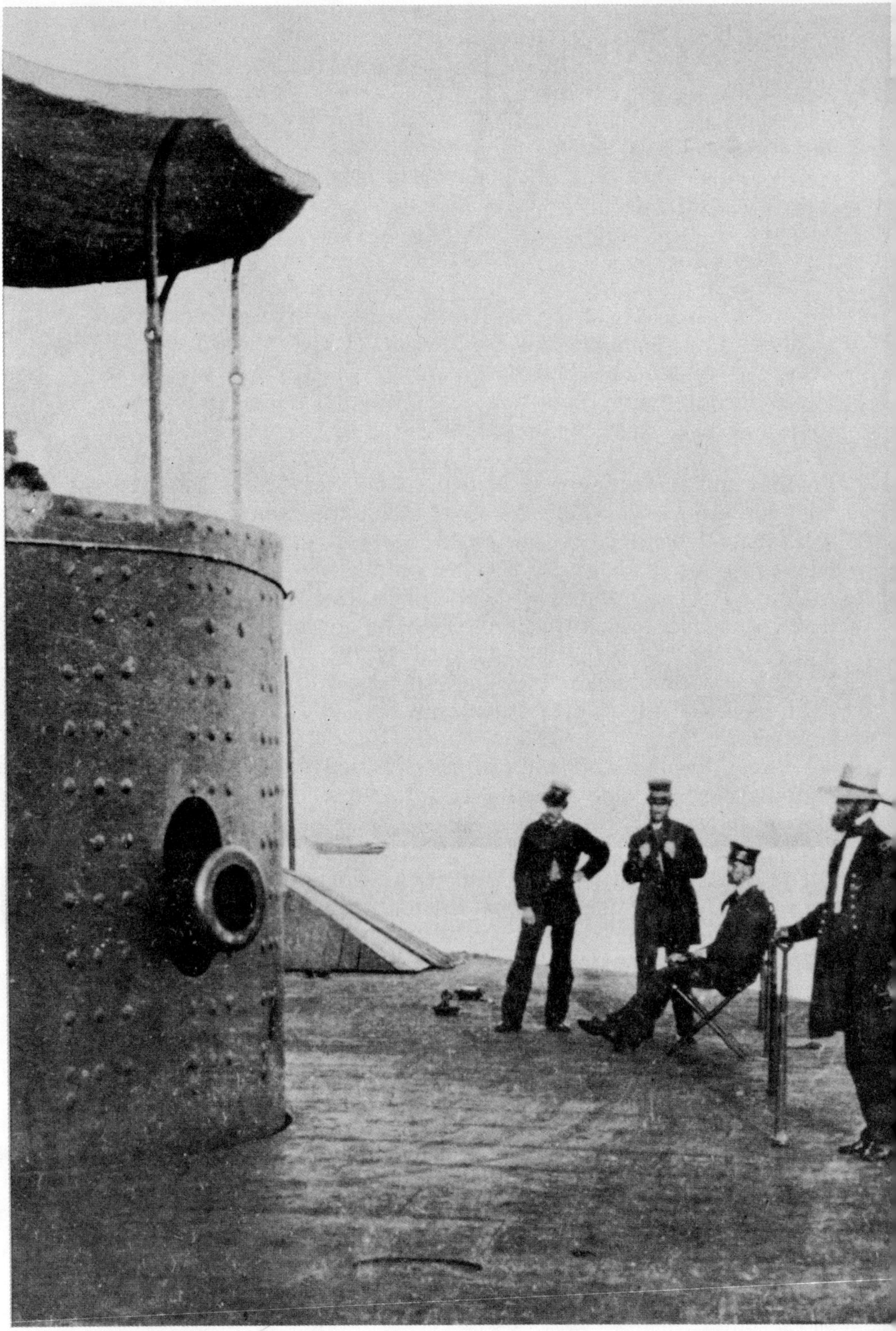

The *Monitor's* crew is photographed by the turret after the famous battle.

The battle of the *Monitor* and the *Merrimac* on March 9, 1862 revolutionized sea warfare, leading to modern battleships. For hours the two ironclads pounded away at one another, sometimes no more than 10 yards apart. Though neither suffered serious damage, they never fought again.

In his white hat, the commander of the *Monitor* inspects the minor damage resulting from its encounter with the *Merrimac*.

acy. "My lord," he concluded icily, "I need hardly remind you that this is war." A belated order to seize the ship reached Liverpool on July 29 – after the "290" had put to sea.

After taking on guns and ammunition at the Azores and mustering a picked crew (chiefly British), the "290" emerged as the *Alabama*. Under Captain Rafael Semmes, a Southerner who before the war had been a U.S. naval officer, this swift Confederate raider nearly drove Northern shipping from the high seas; in two years the *Alabama* captured some 70 vessels (all unarmed merchantmen), burning 57 and releasing the rest under ransom.

In his cabin Semmes kept as trophies the chronometers of the ships he had destroyed – "as proudly exhibited," the *New York Herald* noted bitterly, "as the scalps in the wigwam of an Indian chief." Southerners retorted that Semmes always provided for the safety of the passengers and crew of any vessels he destroyed. One time he approached a foreign port to land several hundred prisoners, but on learning there was yellow fever there he let them go free on a prize he had saved.

For the *Alabama* the end came on June 19, 1864, in the English Channel. Nettled by taunts that his cruiser was not a warship but a pirate ("Semmes has been a wolf of the deep/For many a day to harmless sheep"), the Confederate commander accepted the challenge of Captain Winslow's U.S.S. *Kearsage*. In a spirited duel watched by crowds on the cliffs of the nearby French coast, the Union warship sank the famous raider.

Filling up the regiments: At the start, men in both sections thronged to the colors: the Confederacy's "And live and die for Dixie," was matched by the Union's "As He died to make men holy, let us die to make men free." Patriotism, North and South, was supported by all the forces of public opinion – the press and pulpit, the womenfolk, the poets and orators. Youth predominated; of these youths Emerson wrote:

> So nigh is grandeur to our dust,
> So near is God to man,
> When Duty whispers low, "Thou must,"
> The youth replies, "I can."

Gradually the initial romantic, or idealistic, enthusiasm was replaced by a more sober appraisal of the dangers and hardships, the

The U.S.S. *Kearsarge* engages the Confederate Raider, C.S.S. *Alabama* off the coast of Cherbourg, France on June 19, 1864.

monotony, dirt, disease, and discouragement of life in the field. By 1863, both sides were resorting to the draft, and soon new recruits had to be bludgeoned into the ranks by conscription or wheedled into them by bounties. The ranks were never quite filled. When Early invaded Maryland in the spring of 1864, the War Department received a telegram from General West, then in Philadelphia, inquiring whether he could be of service. Halleck replied, "We have five times as many generals here as we want, but we are greatly in need of privates."

Southern draft dodgers tried to reach a border state which had not seceded while Northerners of that stripe made for Canada. Taking note of the "refugees," a Northern newspaper scornfully hurled at them the lines from Shakespeare's *Henry V*:

> That he which hath no stomach to this fight,
> Let him depart; his passport shall be made . . .

The press also jibed at men in uniform who managed to keep clear of any fighting front. This item appeared as a "filler": "Here's your *Daily Times* – All about the great battle," a newsboy cried. A man in uniform bought a paper, scanned the dispatches, and then demanded, "Where is this about the battle? I can't see it." "No," said the newsboy. "And you never will see it, so long as you hang around this city."

New York City's own civil war: A few days after Gettysburg and Vicksburg violent anti-draft riots erupted in New York City. The conscription law exempted high state and Federal officials, the only son of a widow or aged depended father, the father of motherless children under 12, and the remaining men of a family which had already sent two members into service.

Through some twisted reasoning Congress also provided that a draftee might hire a substitute, or pay the government $300 to provide a bounty for an enlistee. Copperheads and agitators seized upon this provision to inflame the city's workingmen ("A rich man's war and a poor man's fight").

Monday, July 13, 1863, an armed mob wrecked several draft offices, fired other buildings, and attacked the homes of prominent citizens who had supported conscription. ("Hang Horace Greeley to a sour-apple tree," was their favorite cry); they beat up, and even lynched, hapless blacks caught in the streets, and repulsed police and troops. Regiments equipped with artillery finally suppressed the rioting. In four days of violence some 1,000 persons were killed or wounded, and property estimated at more the 1½ million dollars was destroyed.

Northern neutralists and appeasers – the Copperheads: A small, but active, Northern minority which sympathized with the South sought to impede the Union war effort. Proposals for dealing with this disloyal element – termed Copperheads – ranged from expulsion to hanging. Their leader, Clement L. Vallandigham, an Ohio lawyer and politician (Congressman until March 4, 1863), finally was arrested, tried, and sentenced to prison. The President commuted the sentence to banishment to the Confederacy. When Vallandigham's arrest by the military, rather than civil, authorities was criticized, Lincoln replied, "Must I shoot a simple-minded soldier who deserts, while I must not touch a hair of the wily agitator who induces him to desert?"

The Northern press vented its scorn on the Copperheads. Said one journal in July, 1863, "When the news of the victory of General Meade over Lee became fully confirmed, many noted Copperheads in this village took to their holes with elongated visages, and on Tuesday when the capitulation of Vicksburg was announced they drew their holes in after them."

Public opinion and the war: Each great battle was refought in the press and in the halls of Congress – to say nothing of bars, street corners, and country stores. One Lincoln biographer, taking note of the Monday-morning quarterbacks, says that the President "was the most advised man, often the worst advised man, in the annals of mankind."

When friends seemed puzzled because he took advice, criticism, and abuse calmly, Lincoln liked to tell them about henpecked Mr. Jones. One day neighbor Smith said, "Jones, any man who will take a switching from his wife deserves to be horsewhipped." Patting his friend on the back Jones said softly, "Why, it didn't hurt me any, and you've no idea what a power of good it did Sarah Ann."

Though able, experienced, and wholly devoted to the Confederate cause, President Jefferson Davis was impatient of advice and intolerant of criticism. Never very popular, he became in time downright un-popular and in April, 1864, was bitterly attacked by the *Richmond Examiner*. When a copy was shown to Lincoln he said with a chuckle, "Why, the *Examiner* seems about as fond of Jeff as the [New York] *World* is of me."

The Civil War was the first great conflict to be covered adequately by reporters and photographers in the field. The generals sometimes didn't like that, fearing that the correspondents in their zeal for news might disclose valuable information to the enemy. To a reporter who averred he only wanted the truth, General Sherman said, "We don't want the truth told about things here – that's what we don't want."

A unique record of the War was compiled by photographer Matthew Brady, a portrait specialist, who left a profitable business to photograph the conflict – the battlefield and camp, generals and privates, war's pathos and war's heroism. "A spirit in my feet said – go," he told a friend. Soldiers named Brady's portable darkroom "the Whatsit Wagon." Brady spent a fortune taking thousands of on-the-spot photographs, but later managed to rebuild his business; however, branching out also into real estate he went bankrupt, in 1873, and eventually died in a hospital alms ward.

Random shots: A major in the 23rd Regiment Ohio Volunteers came out of the war a brigadier-general and 11 years later was elected President of the United States. An 18-year-old private in the same regiment eventually rose to the rank of major; in time he also became President. The two were Rutherford B. Hayes and William McKinley.

After the Confederates withdrew from the Manassas area (March, 1862) Union troops discovered they had been facing phantom guns; running short of artillery the Confederates had set up wooden imitations of cannon. (On one occasion in World War II our G.I.'s used dummy tanks made of rubber.)

A Confederate inventor built a double-barreled cannon firing round shot linked by a chain, the idea being to mow the enemy down by platoons; however, when the gun was fired the charges failed to go off simultaneously, resulting in a sad tangle of shot and chain.

More successful was the Union's rapid-fire gun designed by Richard Gatling. Unlike the modern machine gun the original Gatling gun consisted of a cluster of barrels firing in rotation. The inventor, a farm machinery manufacturer, hoped that his destructive weapon would help eliminate war.

Of human fortitude: In the battle of Mobile Bay, the U.S.S. *Tecumseh* struck a Confederate mine and sank with 113 of her crew. Just before the ship went down, the pilot and Captain Craven met below

Two future Presidents of the United States, Rutherford B. Hayes (left) and William McKinley (right) fought in the Civil War. Hayes was a brigadier-general at the end of the war. Eleven years later, he was President. McKinley started as an 18-year-old private.

deck at the foot of a narrow ladder. "After you," said the commander. The pilot was saved; the captain was lost with his ship.

Francis Marion Cockrell, who joined the Confederate army as a private and in less than a year became a brigadier-general, was taken prisoner three times and wounded five times. Confederate General Francis Nicholls, who lost an arm at Winchester, returned to active service after a brief furlough and lost a leg at Chancellorsville.

General O. O. Howard, the Union counterpart of the deeply religious "Stonewall" Jackson, had his *right* arm shattered in battle. After its amputation he met General Kearny who had lost his *left* arm in the Mexican War. "I want to make a bargain with you, General," Howard said, "that hereafter we buy our gloves together." (Kearny was killed soon afterward in a minor engagement.)

The generals surely did not stay in their tents, for on both sides the casualties were heavy. This is a partial list: The Confederates lost Albert S. Johnston at Shiloh; "Stonewall" Jackson at Chancellorsville; JEB Stuart in the 1864 Wilderness campaign; Leonidas Polk (one-time Episcopal bishop of Louisiana) in the fighting against Sherman in Georgia; and James Pettigrew near Winchester. Joseph E. Johnston was severely wounded at Fair Oaks, as was James Longstreet in the Wilderness campaign.

On the Union side, besides Kearny, Isaac P. Rodman was mortally wounded at Antietam; John F. Reynolds was killed at Gettysburg; L. H. L. Wallace, at Shiloh; Wadsworth and Sedgwick, in the Wilderness battles; Daniel McCook (one of eight brothers in the Union armies), at Kenesaw Mountain in the advance on Atlanta; and McPherson, at Peachtree Creek in the same campaign.

The cloak and dagger section: At first the Lincoln administration failed to take even elementary precautions to keep vital information from being transmitted to the Confederates. Before the first battle of Bull Run, Washington socialite Mrs. Rose O'Neal Greenhow sent General Beauregard information about the size of McDowell's forces and the time of their march on Manassas. After other services to the South, Mrs. Greenhow was arrested and convicted as a spy; but the charming widow had influential friends in Washington, so she was merely banished to the Confederacy.

The Union counterpart to Mrs. Greenhow, actress Pauline Cushman, was seized with incriminating maps in her possession, and after trial by court-martial at Shelbyville (Tennessee) was sentenced to be hanged. Soon afterward the Union advance compelled General Bragg to retreat, and in the confusion Pauline was left behind.

The men were less fortunate. Timothy Webster, one of the Pinkerton detectives who had uncovered the 1861 plot to assassinate President-elect Lincoln, became a Union spy; he finally was caught, tried, and sentenced to be hanged. As the trap was sprung the knot of the rope became undone. Carried back upon the scaffold Webster cried out, "I suffer a double death." This time the knot held.

Young Sam Davis (the "Confederacy's Nathan Hale") was captured with papers he had obtained from a spy behind the Union lines. Though offered his freedom if he would disclose the source of his information Davis refused and went to his death.

Foreign soldiers and black units: As an aftermath of the revolutions of 1848 and the wars of Italian unification, Europe contained many soldiers of fortune who, out of idealism or love of adventure, were ready to fight again – if someone would pay their passage. In 1862 a group of Americans who were visiting the London Exposition made up a purse to send over four Italians, four Hungarians, three Germans, and one Pole. Of this group only one failed to live up to his pledge to join the Union army.

Henry M. Stanley (later famous as an African explorer) came to New Orleans from Wales. When the war broke out he enlisted in the Confederate army; captured at Shiloh, he switched sides and served as a Federal artilleryman. (Another version holds that he escaped and returned to Wales, then came back to America and enlisted in the Union navy.)

Both sides raised black regiments. The first Union regiment of black troops, the First South Carolina Volunteers, was recruited in the Sea Islands after they came under Federal control; a Kansas black regiment was next. Blacks were included under the Federal 1864 conscription law; in loyal border states where slavery was still legal, the master received a bounty for every slave who was drafted. Tennessee early authorized its governor to enlist black troops, and in 1862 a regiment of 1,400 free slaves entered the Confederate service. In March, 1865, the Confederate Congress passed a bill for arming the slaves; it was too late.

The men around Lincoln: To Henry Adams we are indebted for this vivid description of Secretary of State William H. Seward: "A slouching, slender figure; a head like a wise macaw; a beaked nose; shaggy eyebrows; unorderly hair and clothes; hoarse voice; off-hand manner; free talk, and perpetual cigar." On the other hand, Secretary of the Treasury Salmon P. Chase was tall, portly, and handsome. A wig which Secretary of the Navy Gideon Welles wore, coupled with his habit of working quietly and diligently, gave some Washington politicians the idea he was an old fogy; he was merely a patient, hard-working, and efficient public servant. Short and thickset, with a large head, mass of black hair, and heavy beard, Secretary of War Edwin M. Stanton was an energetic and deeply religious man; he was also egotistical and tactless, and was always threatening to resign if he didn't have his way. Two bright young men who became the President's private secretaries and soon learned to idolize him, John Nicolay and John Hay, later produced the first noteworthy Lincoln biography.

He was a man who loved stories, a good-humored, even-tempered man: "They say I tell many stories," Lincoln once remarked. "I reckon I do, but I have learned from experience that plain people, take them as they run, are most easily influenced through the medium of the broad and humorous illustration than in any other way." Yet, he was aware that for a man in public life a reputation for humor had its dangers.

He would tell how two Northern women were discussing the war. "I think Jefferson Davis is a praying man." "But so is Abraham a praying man," her companion protested. "Yes," the troubled lady admitted, "but the Lord will think Abraham is joking."

Lord Bryce said that much of Lincoln's gift for bolstering the North's confidence was "due to the humorous way he used to turn things, conveying the impression of not being himself uneasy, even when he was most so." But it was his prescription also for preserving his own sanity.

When the President, who had spent many sleepless nights trying to figure out what to do about slavery, summoned his Cabinet for a reading of the Emancipation Proclamation, he began the meeting with a chapter from "Artemus Ward, His Book." After laughing heartily over its crude grotesqueries he turned to his epochal statement.

Lincoln dearly loved a pun. When a telegraph operator handed him a dispatch that Union General Schenck had captured 40 prisoners, all armed with Colt's revolver, he observed with a twinkle that by the next day the newspapers with their customary gift for exaggeration would have the "Colt's" grow into horse pistols.

And he was especially fond of the sly satire clothed in the "hayseed" humor of misspelled and mispronounced words and faulty grammar of Petroleum V. Nasby (David R. Locke of the *Toledo Blade*). Once the President told a delegation, "I am going to write to 'Petroleum' to come down here, and I intend to tell him that if he will communicate his talent to me I will swap places with him."

A man of faith and true humility, a modest unassuming man: "It was the Bible which I saw him reading while most of the household still slept," William Crook (one of the President's bodyguards) later reported. "Man is tallest on his knees," the tallest of all our Presidents remarked, and he was many times driven to prayer by the conviction that his own wisdom and that of his advisers "seemed insufficient for that day."

The four terrible years in the White House strengthened Lincoln's belief in God, and his public utterances (as well as private correspondence) became a testament of faith. Here is a moving paragraph from the *Second Inaugural:* "Fondly do we hope, fervently do we pray, that this mighty scourge of war may speedily pass away. Yet if God wills that it continue until all the wealth piled by the bondsman's two hundred and fifty years of unrequited toil shall be sunk, and until every drop of blood drawn with the lash shall be paid with another drawn with the sword, as was said three thousand years ago, so still it must be said: 'The judgments of the Lord are true and righteous altogether.'"

He detested the ceremonial attached to the office and once said to some old friends who were closeted with him, "Now call me 'Lincoln' instead of 'Mr. President,' and I'll promise not to tell of the breach of etiquette."

Generally, Lincoln was indifferent to the cruel comments (and caricatures) on his appearance. But on one occasion he related a dream to John Hay: That he was in a party of plain people, and as it became known that one of them said, "He [Lincoln] is a very common-looking man"; that he overheard the remark and replied, "The Lord prefers common-looking people – that is the reason He makes so many of them."

As a husband Lincoln was faithful and good-natured, and close friends sometimes teased him about his submissiveness to his wife's show of authority in their domestic life. He would laugh and apply the "Jones story," assuring them that his meekness did him no harm and her much good.

As a parent he was devoted and indulgent. The Lincolns had lost a boy of three, Eddie, in Springfield. When in 1863 a second child, 11-year-old Willie, died of a fever the President was heartbroken. About the same time "little Joe," son of Jefferson Davis, fell to his death from an upper story of the family residence in Richmond. The two bereaved fathers, rival leaders in a bitter civil war, exchanged personal letters of sympathy.

A merciful and compassionate man: In the midst of overpowering burdens, Lincoln would find time not only to intercede for the life of a private, but to examine the condemned man's record. Only in instances of cruelty was he merciless. Cases of cowardice, especially where the offender was a mere youth, he was averse to punishing with death. "It would frighten the poor fellows too terribly to shoot them," he said wryly.

To be sure, the generals had a difficult job maintaining discipline and keeping their armies together, especially after each fresh defeat. One officer complained to the President that his pardon of 24 deserters, all under sentence to be shot, impaired discipline and that mercy to the few was cruelty to the many; sharply Lincoln replied, "General, there are already too many weeping widows in the United States. For God's sake, don't ask me to add to the number." When squint-eyed Ben Butler (a notoriously harsh disciplinarian) asked for the pardon of a man he himself had earlier sentenced to be shot, the President exclaimed: "You? Asking *me* to pardon some poor fellow! Give me that pen!"

With respect to his moving letter to Mrs. Bixby it later developed that the President had not been given the correct facts. This is no longer important; what is significant is Lincoln's reaction:

> Dear Madam, I have been shown in the files of the War Department a statement of the Adjutant-General of Massachusetts

that you are the mother of five sons who have died gloriously on the field of battle. I feel how weak and fruitless must be any words of mine which should attempt to beguile you from the grief of a loss so overwhelming. But I cannot refrain from tendering to you the consolation that may be found in the thanks of the Republic they died to save. I pray that our heavenly Father may assuage the anguish of your bereavement, and leave you only the cherished memory of the loved and lost, and the solemn pride that must be yours to have laid so costly a sacrifice upon the alter of freedom. Yours very sincerely and respectfully . . .

No man in all America was more free from the desire for revenge. In his *Second Inaugural,* when the country at last could plainly hear the death rattle of the Confederacy, the President outlined the noblest program of reconstruction ever offered by a victor. "With malice toward none, with charity for all, with firmness in the right, as God give us to see the right, let us strive on to finish the work we are in, to bind up the nation's wounds; to care for him who shall have borne the battle, and for his widow and his orphan; to do all which may achieve and cherish a just and lasting peace among ourselves and with all nations."

Above all he was a resolute man: The customary emphasis on Lincoln's patience and gentleness and compassion must not obscure the vein of iron in the man. Where a principle was involved – where the fate of the Union was at stake – Lincoln was a masterful man. He once said, "It may as well be understood, once for all, that I shall not surrender this game leaving any available card unplayed." No leader had less of the dictator in him, yet he did not shrink from decisive use of executive powers. When critics charged that his suspension of *habeas corpus* without specific authorization of Congress was a violation of the Constitution, the President replied, "Do you wish me to lose the nation while preserving the Constitution?"

To Horace Greeley of the *New York Tribune* who urged immediate emancipation when Lincoln thought it was too soon for such action, he wrote, "What I do about slavery and the colored race, I do because I believe it helps to save the Union; and what I forbear, I forbear because I do not believe it would help save the Union."

Lincoln might yield to a Cabinet member on a trifle, but never on a vital issue. He was the Cabinet's master not its agent. Secretary of War Stanton sometimes returned a document to the President with the curt note, "The President may get another Secretary of War, but this Secretary of War will not sign that paper." But Lincoln tolerated Stanton's rudeness, bad temper, and tactlessness because he valued his patriotism, honesty, and ability.

He did not allow the war to interfere with the erection of the Capitol's vast new cast-iron dome, for the work was to him a symbol of Union strength, a prophecy of reunion. (When on December 2, 1863, the 20-foot statue of Freedom was raised above the dome it was greeted with a 35-gun salute – one for each state, North *and* South.)

In the heartbreaking series of campaigns against Lee it was Lincoln who repeatedly sought to put starch into the Union generals; but not until Grant took command did he at last have a man who did not need stiffening. "I have seen your dispatch expressing your unwillingness to break your hold where you are," the President told him. "Neither am I willing. Hold on with a bulldog grip and chew and choke as much as possible."

Shortly after Gettysburg, youthful John Hay, shrewd and observant, had written: "The Tycoon [one of his private names for Lincoln] is in fine whack. He is managing this war, the draft, foreign relations, and planning a reconstruction of the Union all at once. There is no man in the country so wise, so gentle, and so *firm*." It was a prophetic flash which anticipated history's verdict.

To return to the battle for Richmond: After three years, the veteran Union Army of the Potomac was encamped, in the spring of 1864, about a day's march from Bull Run where it had fought the first great battle in its drive to take Richmond. Early in May, Grant crossed the Rapidan; Lee advanced to meet him, and the armies met head-on in a tangle of woods and brush known as the Wilderness. Once again Lee's veterans prevented a break-through, but this time the Union army kept pressing. "I propose to fight it out on this line if it takes all summer," Grant informed the War Department. When the Union soldiers discovered that despite setbacks they still faced south, they cheered. The men were tired of retreating – they wanted to get it over with.

In a letter to his family, a veteran of the Wilderness fighting, Private Irving Wood of Michigan, described what he and his comrades endured. "We charged the enemy's works through a thicket of pines but we could not reach them as they had slashed the trees in front. They opened some batteries on us. Grape, canister, shell & musket balls came as thick as rain. It seemed impossible for men to live in those woods. Every tree was riddled and splintered up."

Private Wood was unscathed in the Wilderness inferno, but at Cold Harbor – an unnecessary battle – he was mortally wounded.

The Confederates held a strongly fortified position which Grant attempted to take by direct assault. Before the "zero hour," dawn of June 3, one of Grant's aides observed many of the men pinning to their uniforms slips of paper bearing their name and home address, so that if they fell they might be readily identified and their families notified. In one frightful hour – before the assault was called off – 6,000 Union men were killed or wounded. Cold Harbor was a blunder which Grant did not repeat; thereafter, he kept probing at the thin points in Lee's lines. And though Lee managed to keep from being overwhelmed or outflanked, he could not prevent the steady attrition of his forces. In the meantime, Sherman and Thomas were cutting in from the softer underbelly of the Confederacy.

A pillar of fire by night, a pillar of smoke by day: Early in May, 1864, Sherman marched from Chattanooga in a determined drive on Atlanta, arsenal of the South. By September the city was in Union hands. President Davis did not help the Confederate cause by replacing the resourceful Joe Johnston with the impetuous Hood. Leaving Thomas to engage Hood, Sherman struck out boldly from Atlanta to the sea. With little organized resistance to dispute the advance, the march through fruitful Georgia took on the aspects of a picnic.

"It was not the sound of fife and drum that heralded the approach of Sherman's triumphant army," a Southerner wrote, "but the lowing of driven cattle and the squawking of poultry or squealing of pigs hung from the saddle-bows, or dragged behind the horses of the foragers and bummers." Probably the most popular order ever given any Army was Sherman's "forage liberally on the country." To dry up Lee's chief source of provisions and end the war as quickly as possible, the invaders cut an 80-mile swath of destruction through Georgia. . . . Both Sherman and Grant worried over Thomas's delay in attacking Hood, for while the latter remained in the field there was a possibility that Sherman might be attacked from the rear. But at Nashville (December 15-16) Thomas struck Hood so hard that he shattered the Confederate army. It was the most complete Union victory of the war.

On Christmas Day, 1864, having reached the coast, Sherman sent the President this dispatch: "I beg to present you as a Christmas gift the city of Savannah with 150 heavy guns and plenty of ammunition and also about 25,000 bales of cotton."

THE CIVIL WAR
Where Americans Fought Americans

Like Grant, Sherman also had floundered about before 1861. He fought in the Mexican War and later against the Plains Indians; then, after resigning from the army, he tried business in California and law in Kansas. In July, 1859, he became superintendent of a new military school in Louisiana, but when South Carolina seceded he resigned his post and rejoined the U.S. army. He was as matter-of-fact as his chief; there was a "lick-all-creation" air about him which seeped down and stiffened the back-bone of the humblest private in the army.

Early's raid: That Washington still was not safe, was driven home sharply to the North in July, 1864, when Lee sent Early and 20,000 troops into the Shenandoah Valley.

Striking swiftly, Early's troops reached the Seventh Street road within sight of the new dome of the Capitol. Two divisions hastily sent by Grant arrived just in time, and after some sharp skirmishing Early retreated.

Accompanied by Secretary of State Seward, the President had gone to the outskirts to observe the fighting; and as they crouched behind a parapet, a bullet from a Confederate sharpshooter killed an army surgeon only three feet from them. To get a better view Lincoln climbed the parapet and stood there, his tall figure a clear target. "Get down," a young officer ordered sharply. Quickly complying the President said, "Captain, I am glad you know how to talk to a civilian." The officer was Oliver Wendell Holmes, Jr., who had already been wounded three times in combat. (Holmes survived the war and later became a famous judge; the man who had given President Lincoln a well-merited scolding lived long enough to receive a visit from President Franklin D. Roosevelt.)

Grant now placed General Phil Sheridan in command of the Union forces in the Shenandoah. A pugnacious little Irishman – weighing all of 115 pounds – the 33-year-old cavalryman was described as a "mounted torpedo." At Cedar Creek, on September 19, 1864, after a memorable dash from Winchester to the battlefield, Sheridan turned imminent defeat into complete victory. Washington breathed more easily.

Politics in the midst of war: At first it seemed that Lincoln would have a hard fight to win renomination in 1864, and it was no secret that Secretary of the Treasury Chase was his chief rival. Chase once told a friend that there were two offices he hoped to hold before he died: Chief Justice and President. (He was to achieve the first, but not the second; in all our history William Howard Taft alone won this double honor.)

Since the Secretary was a widower his daughter Kate, wife of a millionaire playboy, Senator Sprague of Rhode Island, acted as his hostess. Mrs. Sprague was young, beautiful – and ambitious. Between her and Mrs. Lincoln there was little cordiality; the President's wife complained that Kate came to White House receptions as a guest and presently was holding court as if she were the hostess.

Lincoln knew that Chase was working assiduously to replace him. "It is very bad taste," the President said to Hay, "but I am determined to shut my eyes to all these performances. Mr. Chase makes a good secretary and I shall keep him where he is. If he becomes President, all right!" Another time Lincoln told this story: "My brother and I were once ploughing on an Illinois farm. I was driving the horse and he was holding the plough. The horse was lazy; but on one occasion he rushed across the field so that I with my long legs could scarcely keep up with him. On reaching the end of the furrow, I found an enormous chin-fly fastened on him and knocked it off. My brother asked me what I did that for. I told him I didn't want the old horse bitten in that way. 'Why,' said my brother, 'That's all that made him go!' Now if Mr. —— has a Presidential chin-fly biting him – and that's what makes his department go – I'm not going to knock it off."

The folks back home took care of the Chase-Sprague chin-fly. In February the Republicans of Ohio (Chase's home state) declared for Lincoln; soon afterwards Rhode Island (Sprague's home state) did the same.

It was suspected that the disgruntled Republican politicians backing Chase all along intended at the last moment to substitute Grant or some other Union general. When Grant rejected their overtures, the anti-Lincoln Republicans turned to Fremont and issued a call for a "mass convention" at Cleveland. About 400 attended, and they had so little knowledge of the Constitution that they nominated two New Yorkers: *General* Fremont for President and *General* Cochrane for Vice President. On being told that only 400 had appeared at Cleveland, Lincoln took up his Bible and read aloud the account of David's forces at the Cave of Adulam (I *Samuel 22:2*): "And every one that was in distress, and every one that was in debt, and every one that was discontented, gathered themselves unto him; and he became a captain over them: And there were with him about 400 men."

The nation decides not to swap horses while crossing the stream: In June, Lincoln was renominated by the Union Party, a combination of Republicans and "war Democrats." The despised nomination for Vice President finally went to Andrew Johnson of Tennessee (a Union Democrat), chiefly because the Convention was anxious to prove that theirs was not a sectional party. It is strange that those who railed most against Lincoln as a "dictator" repeatedly turned to military men to replace him. The Democrats nominated *General* McClellan and called for a cessation of hostilities. So thick was the gloom in the North over Grant's initial failure to crack Lee's lines before Richmond that Greeley declared, "Mr. Lincoln is already beaten." And Mr. Lincoln himself wrote, "It seems exceedingly probable that this Administration will not be re-elected." A string of victories – Farragut's at Mobile Bay, Sherman's at Atlanta, Sheridan's in the Shenandoah – made hash of both opinions. Yet, despite Lincoln's overwhelming electoral vote (212 to 21), the popular vote was fairly close: 2,216,067 to 1,808,725.

Postscript on the men who figured in the 1864 campaign: On a question of patronage Chase resigned from the Cabinet on June 29, 1864 – his fourth, possibly fifth, formal resignation. This time, instead of again persuading him to reconsider, Lincoln quickly accepted; however, before the year was out he sent in Chase's nomination as Chief Justice of the United States. Ben Butler who had turned down the Vice Presidency on the Union ticket, feeling that he was qualified for the top spot, had to wait a long time; but he finally was nominated for the Presidency in 1884 – by the Greenback and Anti-monopoly parties. In later life Fremont had as little success in business as in politics, losing his fortune in railroad ventures. McClellan, after a career as a successful marine engineer, was in 1877 elected governor of New Jersey. Vallandigham (who was received in the Confederacy with such coldness that he soon left for Canada) had returned to Ohio in June, 1864. The government let him stay. In 1871, while representing a defendant in a murder case he was killed by the accidental discharge of a pistol he was exhibiting to the jury.

The beginning of the end: The Civil War was total war, for the Confederacy fought until it no longer could maintain troops in the field. Holding the conflict a rebellion, the North generally would consider no terms save unconditional surrender; but at the Hampton Roads "Peace Conference" (January, 1865) aboard a Federal steamer, Lincoln and Seward did receive three Confederate commissioners. Congress had just proposed the 13th Amendment abolishing slavery. Lincoln said that if the Southern states would lay down their arms and accept "prospective ratification" of the amendment, he would favor a fair indemnity, perhaps 400 million dollars. This in January, 1865, when two Union armies – Grant's in Virginia and Sherman's in South Carolina – were squeezing the remaining life out of the Confederacy! But Davis kept talking continued "resistance to unconditional submission." In an impassioned address the Confederate President (ill and weak at the time) said, "With the Confederacy I will live or die. Thank God I represent a people too proud to eat the leek or bow the neck to mortal man." This was noble – but did it face reality? At that moment Lee was writing that his commissary "had not a pound of meat."

More than meat was in short supply in what remained of the Confederacy. A Union soldier stationed in the Kanawah Valley in West Virginia (a quiet sector) wrote home, "We average 40 deserters per day from the rebel army. They come in all shapes, some almost stark naked wrapped in blankets."

Confederate paper money no longer possessed much value. A Southern housewife noted, "Mr. Petigru says you take your money to market in the market-basket and bring home what you buy in your pocket book." And what was the Congress at Richmond doing in these last critical hours? It was heatedly debating the design of the Great Seal of the Confederacy. Washington was to be the central figure, but state pride prevented agreement on selection of the Southern statesmen and soldiers to surround him.

Appomattox – Grant's finest hour: When the Confederacy's collapse came it was swift and complete, sparing a ravaged land the further horror of protracted guerrilla warfare. On April 3, Grant entered Richmond which he had forced Lee to abandon. Informed by his officers that the Confederate army was encircled, that it had no food and very little ammunition, and that the men were deserting, abandoning their arms in the trenches, Lee said, "Then there is nothing left me but to go and see General Grant (usually he referred to him as "that man"), and I would rather die a thousand deaths."

The two commanders met on Palm Sunday, April 9, at the red brick home of Wilmer McLean in Appomattox Court House. (Earlier McLean had lived on a farm near Manassas. To get away from the clashing armies which twice had turned his land into a battlefield he moved to Appomattox, but the war caught up with him.) Lee wore a full dress uniform of Confederate gray and carried a magnificent sword, the gift of a Marylander living in Paris. Grant had on a dark blue flannel blouse, a private's fatigue-dress uniform to which were sewn the shoulder straps of his rank. He apologized to Lee for not wearing his sword. They talked first about former times – the Mexican War and the old army in which they had been brother officers – and Grant afterward disclosed that he "almost forgot the object of their meeting." There was no haggling: Grant allowed Confederate officers to retain their side-arms and horses; and when Lee pointed out that in his army the calvarymen and artillerists also owned their horses he agreed they should keep the animals "as they would need them for spring plowing." Since Lee hinted that his men were subsisting principally on parched corn the Union commander offered to supply them with rations. The surrender documents signed, they separated. (They met again only once; in 1869 *President* Lee of Washington College happened to be in the Capital and paid a courtesy call on *President* Grant of the United States.) When the glad news reached the Union army some troops prepared to fire a salute, but Grant stopped them; he had done the same after Donelson, his first important victory.

The lost cause: Lee's aide, Captain Ransom, who was among those who greeted the Confederate leader when he returned from his meeting with Grant, later wrote: "General Lee's head was not bowed. He tried to speak to his men but the words stuck in his throat." Sitting on a stump nearby, a general of the Second Army Corps was crying uncontrolledly "as a child will cry." There was a sudden movement toward the flags; soldiers and officers stripped the battle-stained bullet-riddled banners from their staffs and stuffed them under their shirts or jackets.

The following day Captain Ransom, ill and weak from lack of food, was standing guard outside Lee's tent. A Federal officer looked up at the dispirited Confederate soldier, then said, "If I were you I would be the proudest man in the world. When I rode into your lines this morning and saw the poor remnants of the army which had baffled us so long, I was ashamed of myself."

Bow down, dear land, for thou hast found release: When news of Lee's surrender reached Washington, workmen dropped their tools; headed by a band, an informal parade soon wound its way to the White House. Begging to be excused from a serious speech Lincoln explained, "I am going to make a formal address this evening and if I dribble it out to you now, my speech tonight will be spoiled." Then to the band: "I think it would be a good plan for you to play 'Dixie'. I always thought that it was the most beautiful of our songs. I have submitted the question of its ownership to the Attorney General, and he has given it as his legal opinion that we have fairly earned it back." In the afternoon a delegation presented the President with an elaborately framed picture. When he saw it was his own likeness Lincoln smiled broadly. "Gentlemen," he said, "I thank you for this token of your esteem. You did your best. It is not your fault that the frame is so much more rare than the picture."

After Appomattox, remaining Confederate resistance petered out: the last battle was fought on May 13, 1865, in far-off Texas; the last general still in the field, Kirby Smith, capitulated on May 26. On the day of Lee's surrender the Union armies numbered 1,000,516 men, and the speed with which this mighty host was disbanded excited the amazement and admiration of foreigners. The American war spawned no "man on horseback."

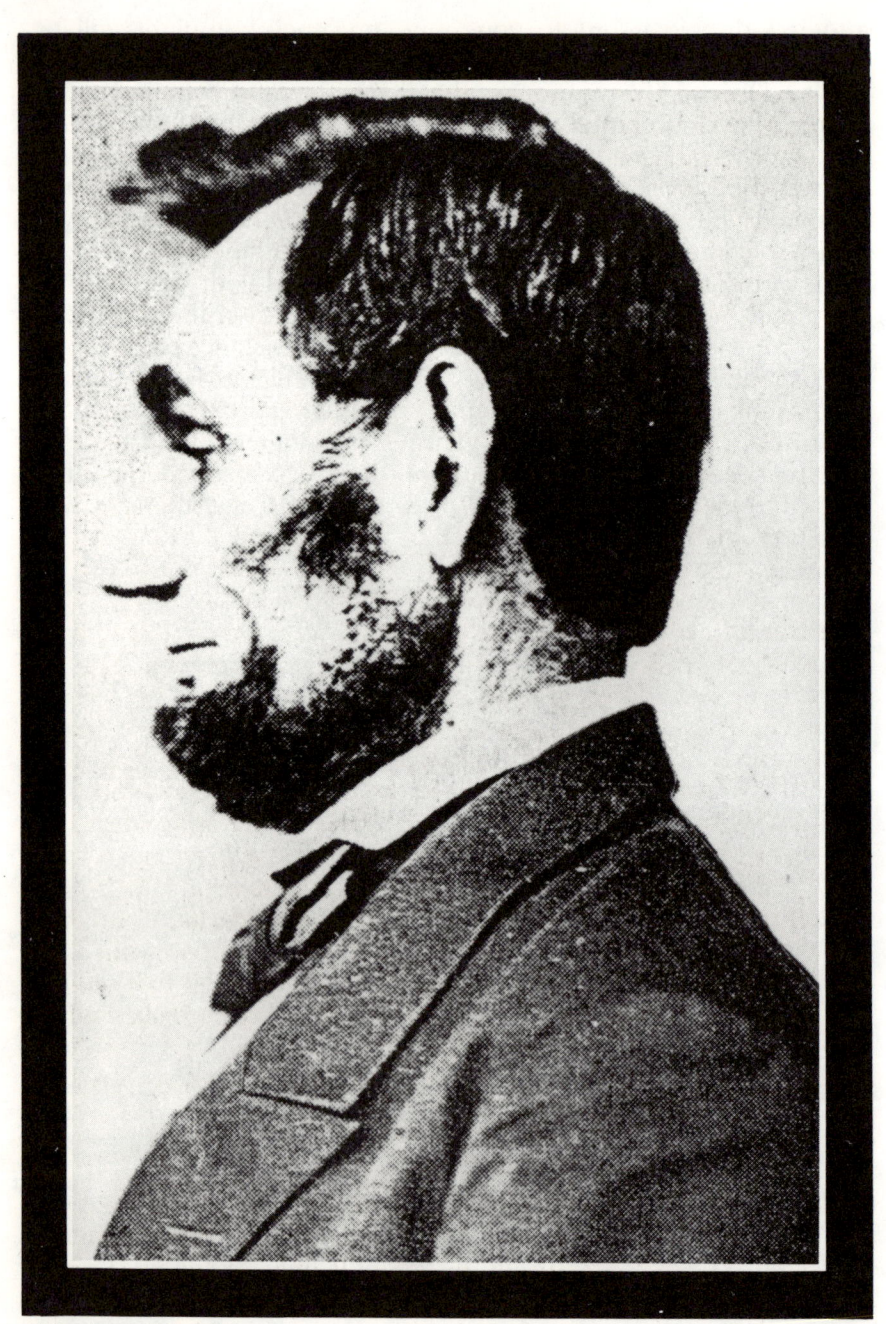

Abraham Lincoln

5

ASSASSINATION AND ATTEMPTED ASSASSINATION

There is many a boy here today who looks on war as all glory, but, boys, it is all hell. You can bear this warning voice to generations yet to come. I look upon war with horror.

– General William T. Sherman's speech to war veterans (1880)

The tragedy of reconstruction: The Civil War was followed by a vengeful sordid decade, "The Age of Hate," or "The Tragic Era." It might have been different had Lincoln lived to complete his second term. The President held that the Federal government had merely been suppressing disloyal groups in certain states, and that as soon as loyal governments were organized their representatives would be readmitted to Congress. Republican politicians had other ideas.

A few hours after Lee abandoned Richmond, the President with a small escort had visited the erstwhile Confederate capital. It was foolhardy, for parts of the city were on fire and dejected Confederate soldiers (some of them drunk) were wandering about, but Lincoln felt his presence would be a gesture of good-will that would help re-unite the sections. When Union General Weitzel asked what he should do "in regard to the conquered people," the President said, "If I were in your place I'd let 'em up easy." His last words to his Cabinet on reconstruction were: "I hope there will be no persecution. . ."

Friday, April 14, 1865: From the moment he was nominated Lincoln's life had been threatened. He shrugged off all threats. To an old friend, Hannah Armstrong, he said, "If they do kill me, I shall never die another death." At Washington, though the threatening letters piled up (later they found a bundle labeled "Assassination Letters") Lincoln opposed any special precautions. But after a shot narrowly missed him when he was out riding one day, he consented to a guard of four police officers in shifts. Following Lee's surrender, however, there was a let-down in safety precautions.

At Ford's Theater on Tenth Street, Washington, that Friday night the curtain went up on the last performance of Taylor's *Our American Cousin*. It had been advertised that the President and Mrs. Lincoln would be present. (His fondness for the theater was well known, and he attended whenever he could.) Lincoln was tired, for it had been an exciting day climaxing an eventful week, but to his wife who urged him not to go, he said, "I cannot disappoint the people."

Later Mrs. Lincoln disclosed that the President seemed to take little notice of the play – once he whispered to her that some day he would take her to the Holy Land, for there was no city he so much desired to see as Jerusalem. Outside the President's box sat the guard of the hour, but lulled by the general belief that the war was over he soon left his post. Shortly after 10 o'clock John Wilkes Booth stole into the President's box, placed a pistol to Lincoln's head, and crying *"Sic semper tyrannis"* (Virginia's official motto) fired.

When Major Rathbone who was in the President's box tried to seize the assassin, Booth struck at him with a knife and then leaped to the stage directly below; but, one of his spurs catching in the folds of the flag draped over the Presidential box, he fell heavily breaking a leg. He rose immediately and, brandishing his knife at the audience, hobbled out of the theater, mounted a waiting horse, and sped away.

A leader passes and is mourned: The assassin's ball had entered the base of the brain, rendering Lincoln insensible. He was carried to the Peterson house across the street from the theater, but never recovered consciousness and died at 7:22 a.m. The audience at the theater had quickly spread the word: a crowd rushed to the White House and shouted the dreadful news to Hay and to Robert Lincoln, the President's son. Others informed Secretary of War Stanton who also hastened to Tenth Street. (When Lincoln breathed his last it was Stanton who said, "Now he belongs to the ages," and ever since historians have speculated whether it was spoken in grief, or relief.)

"God preserve us as a people," was voiced by many a citizen on learning that Lincoln was dead. In isolated towns Lee's surrender was still being celebrated with the ringing of church bells and joyous manifestations when messengers brought the tidings that changed the ringing to tolling and the flags to sable draperies.

Ford's Theater

April 19, the day of Lincoln's funeral in Washington, was a day of national mourning. Two days later the funeral train started for Springfield. In Baltimore, New York, and other cities the casket was drawn through streets black with mourners. At villages, at crossroads, and in the open countryside people waited patiently – at night beside bonfires – to catch a glimpse of the passing train. In mourning Lincoln, the North mourned all its war dead.

For the South, Lincoln's assassination was a disaster second only to defeat; most Southerners realized they had lost their chief advocate in the difficult trials ahead. In Charleston a citizens' committee which asked for the use of Hibernian Hall to express condemnation of the crime, was led by ex-Congressman Aiken, once the largest slave-owner in America. Britain's *Punch* which during the war had lampooned Lincoln in biting cartoons now made public confession:

> Yes, he had lived to shame me from my sneer,
> To lame my pencil and confute my pen –
> To make me own this hind of princes peer,
> This rail-splitter a true-born king of men.

Though little is known about Lincoln's mother, for she died when he was only nine, she has been portrayed as a frontier Madonna. Avoiding sentimentalism, Stephen and Rosemary Benet have penned perhaps the most poignant tribute to mother and son in the entire vast literature on Abraham Lincoln. In their poem the ghost of Nancy Hanks Lincoln, after many years, returns to earth and asks a stranger:

> You wouldn't know
> About my son?
> Did he grow tall?
> Did he have fun?
> Did he learn to read?
> Did he get to town?
> Do you know his name?
> Did he get on?

The criminal, the crime, and the aftermath: John Wilkes Booth, only 26, was an actor, though hardly in a class with his famous older brother, Edwin. A Marylander by birth, and an ardent supporter of the Confederacy (though he did not enlist), John blamed Lincoln for the South's woes. A tippler and melodramatic actor, Booth im-

After shooting President Lincoln, John Wilkes Booth caught one of his spurs in the flag draped over the presidential box as he leaped to the stage.

agined he would be honored "for doing what Brutus was honored for." Instead, he won universal abhorrence for a crime as senseless as it was tragic, and today lies in an unmarked grave.

In Washington it was a night of horror and alarms. At the same hour that Booth shot Lincoln a fellow conspirator, Lewis Payne, attacked Seward. The Secretary of State was recuperating from injuries suffered April 5 when he was thrown from his carriage. Forcing his way into Seward's sick room, the powerfully built Payne stabbed him in the cheek and throat. In attempting to stop him two of Seward's sons and two attendants were wounded, but none of the assailant's wild slashes and stabs struck a vital mark. Two men had hastened to notify Stanton. Outside his residence they encountered a man muffled in a cloak, and when they hailed him he hurried away. They may have scared off a third conspirator, the slow-witted David Herold; at any rate Herold later joined Booth in the flight into Maryland. High on the conspirators' list was Grant. The General and his wife had been invited to join the President's theater party, but they were anxious to visit their children who were at school in Burlington, New Jersey, and had made their excuses.

At Bryantown, Maryland, Booth stopped at the house of Dr. Samuel Mudd, a Southern sympathizer, who set his leg; then the assassin and Herold crossed into Virginia. Soldiers finally cornered them in a barn near Port Royal. Herold surrendered. When the barn was fired, Booth emerged and – contrary to explicit orders – was shot dead. Payne, Herold, and two other conspirators (including Mrs. Surratt in whose boarding-house the plot was hatched) were tried and hanged; four others who were implicated in Booth's getaway were sentenced to prison.

The most dastardly crime in American history is still shrouded in conjecture. Why wasn't the President better guarded? Why wasn't the delinquent guard, John Parker, officially questioned or called as a witness at the trial of the conspirators? How did a broken-legged man manage to evade his pursuers for 11 days? Why wasn't the assassin taken alive when cornered?

An attempt was made to link Jefferson Davis and other former Confederate officials with the crime, though the trial had indicated that none was implicated. When Davis was captured in Georgia on May 10, Northern papers spitefully reported that he had been disguised in "his wife's petticoats, crinoline and dress." Actually, he had on his wife's waterproof cloak which he had picked up in the confusion when the alarm was given. After being imprisoned for two years in Fort Monroe, Davis was released.

At Norfolk (Virginia) a Federal judge had summoned a grand jury which indicted Lee for treason. Grant promptly informed the administration that any trial of the former Confederate commander would violate the pledge he – Grant – had given at Appomattox. By threatening to resign from the army and take the issue to the country he cut the ground from under the blood-thirsty Washington politicians. The indictment against Lee was dropped.

JULY 1, 1938
Reunion Day – College Stadium

1:00 to 2:00 P. M.
Band Concert by U. S. Army Band

2:00 P. M.
Honorable John S. Rice, Chairman, Pennsylvania State Commission, Presiding
Singing of America
Opening Prayer by G.A.R. Chaplain—Rev. Martin V. Stone, Jamestown, New York
Address of Welcome by Honorable George H. Earle, Governor of Pennsylvania
Address of Welcome by Honorable Harry H. Woodring, Secretary of War
Music
Salute of Honor to G.A.R. Commander-in-Chief
Address by G.A.R. Commander-in-Chief, Dr. Overton H. Mennet, Los Angeles, California
Salute of Honor to U.C.V. Commander-in-Chief
Address by U.C.V. Commander-in-Chief—General John M. Claypool, St. Louis, Mo.
Presentation of Commission Members
Prayer by U.C.V. Chaplain, J. J. Methvin, Andarko, Oklahoma
National Anthem

JULY 2, 1938
Veterans' Day

1:30 P. M.
PARADE
Grand Marshal Major General Edward C. Shannon. The street parade will consist of all units from the regular Army camp in full field equipment, uniformed band and drum corps of the American Legion, Veterans of Foreign Wars, United Spanish War Veterans and Disabled American Veterans from Eastern America; State and Federal commissions and distinguished guests.

PROGRAM

75th Anniversary Battle of Gettysburg

FINAL REUNION of the BLUE AND GRAY

Gettysburg, Pennsylvania

June 29 to July 6

1938

ALL PROGRAMS ON EASTERN DAYLIGHT SAVING TIME

Address: National Commander Scott P. Squyres of the Veterans of Foreign Wars
Presentation of citation and medals to winning band and drum corps
Music
Address: National Commander Daniel J. Doherty of the American Legion
Address: National Adjutant Vivian D. Corbly of disabled American Veterans
Drill by Michigan Zouaves American Legion Drill Team
National Anthem
Taps with distant echo

JULY 3, 1938
President and Peace Memorial Day

7:30 A. M.
Military Field Mass in College Stadium

10:00 A. M.
Memorial Services in College Stadium

5:30 to 6:30 P. M.
Band Concert at Peace Memorial by U. S. Marine Band

6:30 P. M.
Dedication of Eternal Light Peace Memorial
Honorable John S. Rice, Chairman Pennsylvania State Commission, Presiding
Salute to The President of The United States
Opening Music by U. S. Marine Band
Opening Prayer by U.C.V. Chaplain—J. J. Methvin
Introduction of Honorable George H. Earle, Governor of Pennsylvania
Music
Introduction of President Franklin D. Roosevelt by Governor George H. Earle
President's Address
Unveiling of Memorial
Closing Prayer by G.A.R. Chaplain, Martin V. Stone
Music

8:00 to 8:40 P. M.
Band Concert by U. S. Army Band—College Stadium

8:40 to 9:00 P. M.
Opening of Aerial Demonstration

9:00 to 9:20 P. M.
Band Concert by U. S. Army Band

9:20 P. M.
Continuation of Aerial Maneuvers. Beginning at dusk the G.H.Q. air force from Langley Field will simulate an attack on Gettysburg with the following forces:
24-A-17A Airplanes
6-B-17 Airplanes (flying fortresses)
18-PB-2 Pursuit dropping flares
The AA guns with searchlights will simulate the defense of the city

(NOTE: The public is warned not to attempt to handle any of the flares, that will be dropped by the airplanes, which fail to function. In the event a flare fails to function Army officials are to be notified of its location for immediate disposal.)

Between June 29 and July 6, 1938, the last reunion of Union and Confederate soldiers was held at Gettysburg. A portion of the official program is shown here.

Index

Adams, Charles Francis, 55
Adams, Henry, 65
Adams, John Quincy, 15
Aiken, Former Representative, 82
Anderson, Maj. Robert, 37
Armstrong, Hannah, 79

Banks, Gen. Nathaniel, 50
Beauregard, Gen. Pierre Gustave
 Toutant de, 37, 39, 64
Beecher, Rev. Henry Ward, 20, 22
Beekham, Mayor (of Harper's
 Ferry), 29
Bell, Gen., 45
Benet, Rosemary, 82
Benet, Stephen, 82
Benton, Sen. Thomas Hart, 16, 17, 23
Birney, James, 13, 14
Bixby, Mrs., 67
Booth, John Wilkes, 30, 80, 82-83
Brady, Matthew, 62
Bragg, Gen. Braxton, 50, 64
Breckenridge, Sen. John, 32
Broadcloth Mob, 14
Broderick, Sen., 30, 31
Brooks, Preston, 24
Brown, John, 14, 28-30
Bryce, Lord James, 65
Buchanan, James, 23, 24, 26, 34-35, 37
Buckner, Gen. Simon, 47
Burns, Anthony, 18
Burnside, Gen. Ambrose E., 42
Butler, Gen. Ben, 48-49, 67, 74
Butler, Sen. Benjamin, 24

Calhoun, Sen. John C., 10, 16, 17
Carson, Kit, 23
Cass, Lewis, 33
Cato Revolt, 14
Catton, Bruce, 47
Chaffee, Dr., 25
Chase, Salmon P., 12, 65, 72-74
Clay, Sen. Henry, 11, 16-17
Cobb, Rep. Howell, 13
Cochrane, Gen., 73
Cockrell, Francis Marion, 63

Crandall, Prudence, 15
Craven, Capt. (of U.S.S.
 Tecumseh), 62-63
Crittenden, George, 34
Crittenden, Sen. John J., 34
Crittenden, Thomas, 34
Crook, William, 66
Cushman, Pauline, 64

Dana, R.H., 51
Davis, Jefferson, 17, 33, 61, 65, 67,
 70, 75, 84
Davis, "little Joe" (son of Jefferson
 Davis), 67
Davis, Sam, 64
Dent, Julia, 51
Doubleday, Abner, 37
Douglas, Sen. Stephen A., 17, 21,
 26, 32, 35
Douglass, Frederick, 15, 29

Early, Gen. Jubal A., 72
Emerson, Dr. John, 25
Emerson, Ralph Waldo, 11, 14, 17, 58
Ericsson, John, 54
Everett, Edward, 7, 46

Farragut, Adm. David G., 55, 74
Field, Stephen J. (Associate Justice,
 U.S. Supreme Court), 31
Fillmore, Millard, 7, 21
Foote, Sen. Henry S., 16
Forrest, Gen. Nathan B., 47
Fremont, Jessie, 23
Fremont, John C., 23, 73-74

Garrison, William Lloyd, 14, 28
Gatling, Richard, 62
Gorsuch, Dr., 19
Grant, Ulysses S., 47-51, 69, 70,
 72-76, 83-84
Greeley, Horace, 14, 31, 60, 68, 74
Greenhow, Mrs. Rose O'Neal, 64
Grimke, Sarah and Angelina, 13

Hammond, Sen. James H., 31

Hancock, Gen. Winfield Scott, 45-46
Hanks, Nancy, 82
Hart, A.B., 12
Hay, John, 38, 42, 65, 67, 69, 73, 80
Hayes, Rutherford B., 62-63
Helper, Hinton R., 15
Herold, David, 83
Highet, Prof. Gilbert, 47
Holmes, Oliver Wendell, 33, 72
Hood, Gen. John B., 70
Hooker, Gen. Joseph "Fighting Joe", 42-43, 45
Houston, Sam, 17
Howard, Gen. O.O., 63
Hunley, H.L., 55

Jackson, Andrew, 33
Jackson, Gen. Thomas J. "Stonewall", 41, 43, 45, 63
Jefferson, Thomas, 9, 13
Jewett, J. P., 20
Johnson, Andrew, 74
Johnston, Gen. Albert S., 48, 63
Johnston, Gen. Joseph E., 39, 43, 63, 70

Kearny, Gen. Philip, 63
Kelly, Judge, 31-32

LaFollette, Sen. Robert M., 17
Lee, Gen. Robert E., 30, 41, 43, 45-46, 53, 61, 69-70, 72, 74-76, 79-80, 84
Lincoln, Abraham, 26-28, 31-32, 34-35, 37-39, 41-43, 46, 49-51, 53, 61, 64-69, 72-74, 76-80, 82-83
Lincoln, Eddie, 67
Lincoln, Mrs. Mary Todd, 73, 80
Lincoln, Nancy Hanks, 82
Lincoln, Robert, 80
Lincoln, Willie, 67
Locke, David R., 66
Longfellow, Henry Wadsworth, 30
Longstreet, Gen. James, 63
Lovejoy, Elijah P., 14

Lovejoy, Owen, 31
Lowell, James Russell, 33, 53
Lyell, Charles, 11

Macon, Sen., 10
Madison, James, 9
Martineau, Harriet, 12
Mason, James M., 52-53
Maury, Matthew F., 55
May, Rev. Samuel J., 18
McClellan, Gen. George B., 41, 74
McClure, A.K., 48
McCook, Daniel, 63
McDowell, Gen. Irvin, 39, 41, 64
McKinley, William, 62
McLean, Mrs. Eugene, 32-33, 36, 39
McLean, Wilmer, 75
McPherson, Gen. James B., 63
Meade, Gen. George G., 43, 46, 61
Mott, Lucretia, 14
Mudd, Dr. Samuel, 83

Nasby, Petroleum V., 66
Nicholls, Gen. Francis, 63
Nicolay, John, 65

Owen, Mary, 28

Parker, John, 84
Payne, Lewis, 83
Pemberton, Gen. John C., 50
Pettigrew, James, 63
Pickett, Gen. George E., 45-46
Pierce, Franklin, 21
Polk, Leonidas, 63
Pope, Gen. John, 41
Preston, Col., 30

Ransom, Capt. (aide to Gen. Robert E. Lee), 76
Rathbone, Maj., 80
Raventhal, Henry, 12
Reeder, Gov. (Kansas Territory), 22
Reynolds, John. F., 63
Rodman, Isaac P., 63
Roosevelt, Franklin D., 72

Rosecrans, Gen. William S., 50
Ruffin, Edmund, 37
Russell, British Foreign Secretary, 55, 58
Rutledge, Ann, 28
Rutledge, Edward, 9

Sanford, John, 25
Schenck, Gen., 66
Scott, Dred, 25-26
Scott, Gen. Winfield, 21, 51
Sedgwick, Gen. John, 63
Semmes, Capt. Rafael, 58
Seward, William H., 17, 31, 34, 53, 65, 72, 74, 83
Sheriden, Gen. William T., 47, 50, 62-63, 70, 72, 74-75
Slidell, John, 52-53
Smith, Gen. Charles F., 47
Smith, Gerrit, 14, 18
Smith, Kirby, 77
Sprague, Kate (nee Chase, Katherine), 73
Sprague, Sen. William, 73
Stanley, Henry M., 64
Stanton, Edwin M., 41, 65, 68-69, 80, 83
Stedman, Edmund C., 30, 42
Stowe, Harriet Beecher, 20
Stuart, Gen. J.E.B. (James Ewell Brown), 30, 63
Sumner, Sen. Charles, 24
Surrat, Mrs. Mary E., 83

Taft, Sen. Robert A., 17
Taft, William Howard, 73
Taney, Roger B. (Chief Justice of U.S. Supreme Court), 25-26
Taylor, Gen. Zachary, 51
Terry, Judge (of California Supreme Court), 30-31
Thomas, Gen. George H., 43, 50, 70
Thompson, C.W., 14
Thompson, George, 14
Todd, Mary (see also Lincoln, Mary Todd), 28
Toombs, Sen. Robert, 33
Turner, Nat, 15

Vallandigham, Clement L., 61, 74
Victoria, Queen, 53

Wadsworth, Gen., 63
Wallace, Gen. L.H.L., 63
Washburne, Rep. Elihu B., 47
Washington, George, 9
Webster, Sen. Daniel, 17
Webster, Timothy, 64
Weitzel, Gen., 79
Welles, Gideon, 65
West, Gen., 60
Whittier, John Greenleaf, 11, 13, 14, 17, 22
Wilkes, Charles, 52-53
Wilmot, David, 14
Winslow, Capt. John A., 58
Wood, Pvt. Irving, 69-70

GHOST SHIP
The Confederate Raider Alabama

Norman C. Delaney

It has been one hundred and twenty-five years since the C.S.S. *Alabama* fought and lost her dramatic duel with the U.S.S. *Kearsarge*. Only recently, however - in 1984 - divers identified the *Alabama* in 180 feet of water, approximately 4 miles off the coast of France. It seems only a matter of time before cannon and other *Alabama* artifacts will be salvaged, preserved, and exhibited to the public. Because of their historic ties to the famous raider, three nations — the United States, Great Britain, and France — all have a strong interest in salvaging her.

From her beginning, the *Alabama* was truly international. Specially designed by Confederate naval agent James Dunwoody Bulloch as a swift greyhound of the seas, she was built in England by masters of the shipbuilders' craft. Her officers and crew included Englishmen, Southerners, and even men from New England.

Her dedicated captain — Raphael ("Old Beeswax") Semmes, C.S.N. — did much to help create the *Alabama* legend. She earned the titles "ghost ship" and "terror of the seas" by destroying millions of dollars worth of Northern commerce, and engaging and sinking the United States warship *Hatteras*. When she herself finally was sunk by the U.S.S. *Kearsarge*, thousands of spectators at Cherbourg witnessed the event. Her legend continues. The story of the "ghost ship" is timeless; it is one of courageous men at war.

ISBN: 0-913337-15-3
$9.95

The Southfarm Press, P.O. Box 1296, Middletown, CT 06457